98° IS BOILING HOT!

With their latest release, they've become the new "it" band. And *Because of You*, they're getting even hotter! This awesome story follows the amazing journey of four all-American cuties who've turned up the heat on the music scene—and turned it on its head! You'll get up close and personal with all the guys to see how they make their music, what kind of girls make their hearts beat faster, and what the future holds for **98°**!

98°...

And Getting Hotter!

KRISTIN SPARKS

St. Martin's Paperbacks

98° AND GETTING HOTTER

Copyright © 1999 by Kristin Sparks.
Cover photograph © London Features/Anthony Cutajar.

ISBN: 0-312-97200-8

Printed in the United States of America

St. Martin's Paperbacks edition/April 1999

10 9 8 7 6 5 4 3

Acknowledgments

Thanks, God!

Also a big shout out to editors Joe Veltre and Erika Fad, and agent Jimmy Vines. 98° fans are the best—and three of them helped especially. They are: Krystle Zalamea, Kelly Peterson and Angela DiCorpo.

Most of all I'd like to thank Ali Ryan of the Vines Agency, without whom . . .

Heat It Up!

If you love good music, you now have four new friends.

I'm happy to tell you that all you need to be close to your new friends is a CD player and a stereo and some pictures to help you visualize—and a couple of unbelievably wonderful compact discs. (Oh, sure, this book helps lots—but, let's face it, the music comes first. The music is the language your friends communicate with best.)

It's night. It's cold and lonely outside, and you feel . . . Well, you feel sad. You need someone to talk to, but it's too late. . . . Anyway, you don't know what to say. You just want to be with somebody . . . to listen to their breath, their heartbeat . . . to know that you're not alone in the world, and that there are other feelings out there . . . pain, love, delight, sadness, joy.

You tuck yourself into bed. You slip on your headphones.

And there they are!

Their names are Nick, Jeff, Justin and Drew.

They're the new pop and R-and-B group known as 98°.

They've got such nice voices, too, and as those voices sweep against you, sometimes softly, and sometimes with an insistent beat that gladdens your heart, you notice how rich and smooth they are—and how gorgeously they blend together, like the ingredients in a comforting cup of hot chocolate.

Ah, it sounds so nice. . . .

And you feel so much better as they lay down the fragrant

and sweet sounds of such songs as "Because of You," "Invisible Man," "The Hardest Thing" and "True to Your Heart."

And as you listen, you relax, and you don't feel so lonely anymore, because you've been comforted. Comforted by the companionable warmth of these guys, the touch of their voices and way they look at you from the album covers . . .

They know what it's like to feel bad and to feel good.

And they want to share the tears and the laughter with you through that most wonderful of human arts—music.

Got some time?

Put their CDs on. That would be *98°* and *98° and Rising* so far, but there's some classic and modern R and B we'll be talking about later on that would be a nice way to get to know why they're singing this way, and how they learned to do it.

Okay. Got a steaming, fragrant cup of herb tea?

Are those stunning harmonies swirling?

I want you to meet four terrific guys.

Jeff Timmons, Nick Lachey, Justin Jeffre and Drew Lachey.

They're funny, they've got personality to spare, they're entertaining. . . . And talented? Whew!

98° want to sing for you. . . . No group has appreciated new friends more. . . . ever. And no group has ever been so eager to let you know about the kind of music they sing . . . and love so much.

Comfy?

Let's get warm with 98°!

98° of Closeness

Pop music is back.

Hanson and the Spice Girls were early warning signs in 1997 but, in 1998, the *Billboard* charts started really shaking with the coming of the Backstreet Boys, 'N Sync, Five, Boyzone and other groups of young-guy singers who sang, danced, looked cute (or maybe even a little goofy sometimes) and sang bright melodies with lots of harmony. These guys were dubbed *boy bands* by the music press. MTV called their arrival perhaps the most significant music news of the year.

It's ironic, but '98 was also the year of 98°.

Jeff Timmons, Nick Lachey, Justin Jeffre and Drew Lachey are a group. They sing, dance, look cute (but hardly ever goofy) and sing melodies and harmonize.

But are they a boy band?

Well, you'll have to be the judge of that.

Me, I think they could have made it whether or not 1998 was the year of boy bands for reasons I hope will be made clear in this book.

Certainly, they don't particularly like to be called a "boy band"—but they do love their fans, and love the attention their music is receiving on the pop scene.

Some critics lump 98° in with the Backstreet Boys and 'N Sync. This is convenient labelling, but isn't exactly the case.

When asked in an Asian web chat what they thought of the Backstreet Boys, the guys of 98° were quick to give their thoughts:

"We think they are very nice guys," Justin Jeffre replied. "But very different from 98° and we wish them best of luck.

Nick Lachey said, "I like them, (and) think they're good. People like to compare us but we're very different groups."

What are the qualities of boy bands, that are so disliked?

Well, often such bands are manufactured, like New Kids on the Block or Menudo. And there is that eternal sixties image of cute guys lip synching their pop songs and performing well-greased dance numbers amidst a bunch of screaming girls.

That's not the way 98° see themselves at all.

"We formed on our own," Drew told *Teen Machine* magazine, "(We) have fans from age four to 54, perform and sing live at our shows. This boy band labelling doesn't sit well with us at all."

So who are 98°, really?

They are a R-and-B group in the classic style, modern, yet with all the trappings of great artists gone by. Like their idols, Boyz II Men, they are becoming successful because they have such style and class, such wonderful talent, to put across a kind of music developed over a century of song styling.

That doesn't mean they can't be themselves, though. That doesn't mean they can't have a terrific time singing the music they love ("There's no life outside music" Jeff told *Teen Machine*.) and seeing the world—and making a difference in the world.

But enough of all this seriousness. They're be plenty of that later on, along with facts and figures and information you'll be glad you took the time to discover here.

Exactly what is 98°, anyway—and where did they come from?

With a huge 98 sculpted in balloons behind them, the group called 98° sing their monster hit song "Because of You" on the *Donny and Marie Show*. Wearing loose pants and long shirts, they look cool and relaxed, pretty astonishing for what had to be a year filled with hard work as well as excitement.

The backup instruments are canned, but the voices are live.

This must be the tape they've been singing along with all autumn as they travelled around the globe, promoting their new album *98° and Rising*.

Here's Nick Lachey holding his wireless mike with the timeless grace of a true crooner. He's got short hair and a strong chin and dimples. He's slender, with big shoulders and a wholesome look. As he sings the praise of his love, he looks like a well-scrubbed football player. He's got that mike now like a quarterback about to pass for a touchdown. If *GQ* had to choose between the guys for a solo cover to model suits, they'd probably choose Nick Lachey. He's a glamorpuss plus—and he's got the kind of voice that melts hearts—sweet but full of years of soul stylings and gospel passion.

The guys' choreography is spare but effective. Okay, here's Jeff, taking the lead chores. Jeff Lachey, with dark hair and piercing eyes—a higher voice than Nick, the kind of voice that can swoop around a song like Whitney Houston taking her time to exercise her larynx between words of a song. Jeff's the guy who started 98°, but he doesn't act like the boss. With his clean-cut good looks and trim body, he's more like a sturdy member of a team. He's got decades of R-and-B phrasing in that voice and, as he gets his lead licks in, staring at the camera, even though it's just TV, it's almost like he's singing straight from the heart. Directly to you. Jeff's like that. He likes to come down into the audience. Serenade. Get close to the girls who adore him.

As the catchy tune unwinds, the guys do some Temptations steps, and the camera goes to Drew Lachey. Drew's the youngest of the group, and possibly the cutest, in a sparkly-eyed way. And sure enough, there's the baseball cap. Drew's always got some sort of cap on and now, as usual, it's on backwards. Drew's singing backup baritone and he can't help but smile as the girls in the audience scream with excitement at being so close to this great sound, this tight-dancing, sweet soul group. And don't you worry none, parents, if one of his young fans keels over from this experience. Drew's the teen idol to be close to: he's a trained emergency medical technician. Thousands of young girls dream about Drew's mouth-to-mouth resuscitation technique.

Finally, looking way into the whole thing, is Justin Jeffre, laying down the bass line. Justin's been singing and hamming it up since he can remember. He's the class cutup, the party guy, with a friendly oval face and bright friendly eyes, looking for attention and glorying in the fact that finally, *finally*, girls are chasing after him. And the way he dances and sings sells you on the fact that unlike his hero, James Brown, he's not the Hardest Working Man in Show Business. No, he's Happiest Man in Show Business. Justin's dancing and singing and having fun, fun, fun.

When the guys finish, they look thrilled, like they can't quite believe the excited screeches of their young fans. Dick Clark, executive producer of the show (Yes, Dick Clark who's been doing the teenage dance thing since the fifties) comes out with Donnie and Marie Osmond. He's holding a surprise for the guys of 98°. It's a gold record. No, it's not for *98° and Rising*. That album went gold weeks ago, and the guys got their gold at a special ceremony at Motown Cafe in New York City. Nope. This gold record is for the soundtrack for *Mulan*, the Disney full-length animated movie hit of the summer, which featured these four guys from Ohio singing with Stevie Wonder (Stevie Wonder!) a mainstay of Motown and a personal deity to these R-and-B fans. The song is "True to Your Heart."

They look thrilled and excited at the honor, 98° do, and they profusely thank Dick Clark and answer a few questions, admitting that they enjoy the attention of their female fans, but feel a little humble about the whole thing.

As they go on to sing "True to Your Heart" with Donny Osmond, something comes to me. Something clicks. I'm researching these dudes now, studying the kind of music they're singing . . . I've seen and heard the other so-called boy bands—'N Sync and Backstreet Boys and Five—and there's something about this group that's, like, totally different.

And then it comes to me.

I scramble through my notes.

Yes. There it is.

In the *Oxford Dictionary of Popular Music*, in the section about doo-wop (a kind of music that clearly has influenced 98°, and which they perform extremely well) the entry states:

''Doo-wop belonged to an era when a certain politeness and sweetness still lingered in pop performance.''

That's it! I thought. That's what these guys have that no one else has! Not only are they elegant and charming and wear nice clothes and are well-groomed (but of course in a way cool way)—but when they sing and dance, not only are they good at it . . .

They're somehow polite and sweet, but in no way saccharine or corny.

It's obvious from their music that they're having as much fun and joy as any of their fans. And in their interviews they come across as regular guys—honest, nice guys—who are having the time of their lives and giving their thrill right back to their audiences and fans everywhere.

I wish I could tell you that this is the number-one group in the world, that their singles have reached number one always, that their new album is riding the top of the charts, beating out even Garth Brooks.

I can't.

Instead, what I can tell you is that there is a very good chance that soon, very soon indeed, that's going to be the case.

In the meantime, what I can tell you is that these guys have lots of top-ten songs. They've got gold and platinum records . . .

And they've got the talent and dedication to be entertaining people for a long time to come.

Why? Well, for one thing they've always been doing it. These guys have been entertaining people with their singing since they were kids. It's not just a way to get attention and make money for Nick and Jeff, Drew and Justin. It's in their blood. It's a way they express themselves.

"We're actually very romantic guys and it's important for us to do love songs," Justin told *Lime* magazine

For another, they've chosen a wise road. They've chosen music that lasts, and a singing style that won't date. They dress in a way that won't appear dated and weird in a few years. They're going up a curve that's not going to peak for a long time.

They love music—and not just R and B.

"I personally like everything from jazz to gospel to rock and even classical and country," Justin Jeffre pointed out to an Asian interviewer. "I think that's what makes our music well-rounded."

Now, it's true that a great many of their fans are young girls, and that they are enjoying status as teen idols. And why not?

In a piece in the December 19, 1998 *New York Times*, in a review of the Jingle Ball at which 98° appeared, Ann Powers points out "Teenagers use pop stars as role models and channels of desire. They judge artists on their ability to reflect and amplify their own budding emotions without seeming too corny or manipulative. This talent for becoming an imaginary friend is as important to pop success as musical skill."

98° wins on both counts here, and we'll be talking about both.

For one thing, they just shine through not only as great guys, but down-to-earth guys.

In researching this book, I spoke to a fan who has met them and has met 'N Sync and Backstreet Boys. Impassioned, she tells me that, while those other guys are kind of aloof, the 98° guys are friendly and approachable. Funny and engaging, they are thrilled and excited that what they do—sing!—is so appreciated by so many.

And they have picked up some pretty outrageous fans around the world! When asked what the strangest things that fans have done, Drew told an Asian web chat: "Five fans in England took 98° stickers and strategically placed them on their bodies and flashed us on stage."

Some girls have gotten 98° tattoos, and many drive fourteen or fifteen hours to see one of their shows.

Last year, when the group played Montreal, the *Montreal Gazette* reported some of the reasons why these 98° are so adored by their fans:

"Their rhythm-and-blues music is really great and they are soooo handsome," a fan named Quimet said, "And their harmony is to die for."

Another older fan (at twenty-nine, no teen fan!) talked about the support for the band. "It was really, really worth it," she said. "We've done it before for the Backstreet Boys, but these guys are even better," said Natalie Lachance. "They do fabulous rhythm and blues."

In the article, an associate of the group, Paul Jessop, pointed out another amazing aspect of 98°. "They are really nice to their fans. They'll call the girls who hand them their phone numbers—just to say hi."

They also do their very best to answer their fan mail.

But, of course, first and foremost is their music.

It was the music that took Jeff Lachey, years ago, from his college all the way out to Los Angeles. It was the music he loved to listen to and loved to sing. It was the music that kept him going for those years, when members of his first group, Just Us, became discouraged and left. It was the vibrant and emotion R-and-B music that Jeff heard coming over the phone, when he called to Nick Lachey to see if he'd be interested in joining in the cause; the music that made Justin Jeffre leap at the chance of coming to L.A. and singing at the invitation of Jeff and Nick; the music that made Nick's little brother, Drew, drop his perfectly good job in Brooklyn as an EMT to travel to Los Angeles and take scut work to support himself and the band while they worked to find a break.

Yes, it was the music that caused diehard Boyz II Men fan Jeff to go to that fateful concert in L.A. to sing their way backstage—and caused the most astonishing course of events in their young lives.

Yes, and that music is R and B, and it's no fad. It's been around for a while, and its emotional strength will keep it around for a long time. It's the voice of pain and passion of the excluded, and the minorities who have grown strong and proud in adversity—and who can guide us all with their dreams and their hopes and loves.

In a way, their name says it all:

"We threw out a lot of bad names before we came up with 98°..." Drew told *Lime* magazine. "Very bad nàmes like Next Issue, Just Us, Inertia, Verse Four... Then somebody came up with Body Heat and everybody put in their two cents (and came up with) 98°, which is our body temperature in Fahrenheit. We wanted a name that would represent the atmosphere our music creates—think heat, love and passion."

98°: Boy band?

I don't think so.

Joy band?

Definitely.

We're going to talk more about their world. About their music and their label and the people who've influenced them.

But first let's check these hotties out.

First we'll find out how they got their start.

And then we'll get to know what kind of guys they are individually, up close.

Legend of a Band

L.A. hums.

Los Angeles, California sings.

Although, during the day, as the sun beats down and the waves crash against the Pacific shore, this is a city of discordance—phone calls, freeways, cars, hustle, buzz and showbiz—the music of the L.A. night is sweet harmony. Stars and moon and glittering hotspots.

It was on just such a night, at just such a hotspot, that the sizzling career of the band called 98° began.

Can you imagine what it must have been like to be Jeff Timmons on a certain L.A. night?

Boyz II Men—one of his favorite groups, ever—was putting on a concert at a local theater.

Yes, Jeff was excited about hearing Boyz II Men do their R-and-B vocal gymnastics in front of a cheering crowd. The Boyz always put on a good show.

But Jeff Timmons had something else on his mind.

Jeff had a vocal group, and the other guys were with him at that Boys II Men gig. They had the same idea, but they were probably nervous, too. I mean, wouldn't you be, if your goal that fateful evening was nothing less than to give some of what you'd gotten from Boyz II Men back to them.

Like, some music?

Sure, Jeff, the second lead tenor of this spanking new unsigned and unknown group probably also wanted to make contact. Sugarplum fantasies probably danced in his head. If he and his posse—Nick Lachey on lead tenor, Drew Lachey piping in the baritone, and Justin Jeffre holding down the fort with bass—could just get the ears of the Boyz, let rip maybe with a Temptations medley or do a little Four Tops, why, maybe the Boyz would say: Hey! You sing pretty good for white guys!

And then what would happen?

Well, one can only imagine the visions percolating in Jeff's head.

A chance to be a warmup for a Boyz II Men show!

Contact with agents and managers that would get them in front of record companies.

Platinum records!

Stardom!

Thousands of screaming fans!

All the Skyline Chili he could eat!

Well, probably not the last. (Skyline Chili is one of Jeff's fave eats, but we'll get into that a little bit later.)

Fame and fortune? Well, maybe. Right now, though, a few gigs would be nice and a little money. The guys lived together in a cramped L.A. apartment and, for one thing, it would be nice to make a little bread singing, instead of holding down jobs like delivering Chinese food or being a security guard or landscaping.

Can you imagine what it must have been like for Jeff and the guys that night? There must have been butterflies flapping around in their empty stomachs as they watched the Boyz serenade the audience with rhythm-and-blues vocal magic. How many times must it have entered their young minds:

We can't do this! Let's just go home! Let's just forget this craziness!

But if 98° has one other thing besides heat and tight harmony style, it's pluck, pizzazz and good ol' homefried *chutzpah*.

They were intent upon their goal: They were going to get backstage and meet the Boyz, and then they were going to sing to them.

They knew they were good. They had beautiful voices but,

more than that, they had hard work, constant practice and a new kind of idea about how four guys could make soulful, emotional music.

Exactly how Jeff and the team made it backstage is shrouded in the mists of time. With these guys, it might have been something out of a Jim Carrey movie (Okay, Justin, start using that voice of yours to make the guards think it's an Earthquake! Drew, you faint. Nick, do your Mighty Joe Young imitation. I'll volunteer to run backstage and get a doctor—then let you guys in after me!)

Anyway, they got backstage.

Ever been backstage at a theater? One can imagine as the guys, probably dressed in their best dude duds, looked around hopefully for the Boyz as roadies and hangers-on worked and hung out near ropes, pulleys, snack and drink tables. There's probably a guy hauling a cable past them. The smell of excitement and fresh-delivered pizza in the air. Groovy clothes are everywhere, and inside the clothes are important people.

But which ones to talk to?

Well, knowing the guys, they probably shmoozed with everyone, looking like they belonged. It probably didn't take long for the secret to get out that hey, we're singers, too, and 98° will harmonize before you can say whoa! Before they knew it, they were probably talking to lots of people and . . .

Well, it's a fact that a radio DJ from a local station heard them. Here was a great-sounding bunch, singing *a cappella* (Learn this term—you'll see it lots in here. It's Italian for "without accompaniment." Which means just voices.)

Singing *a cappella*, of course, means no heavy equipment to carry around, so, the DJ said, Yo, guys! Why don't you come on my show and blast your wondrous pipes on the airwaves!

In other words, he wanted them to sing on his show.

98° didn't have to be persuaded to do this, of course. They were already singing around town, at auditions and open mikes, and even baseball games. On the air? For thousands of listeners?

Sure.

The funny thing about that breakthrough night was that Boyz II Men never came through that area, and the chums of 98° never got to meet them, much less sing to them.

However, there was this other guy around who heard them and talked to them. He was the assistant manager for super-popular R-and-B artist Montell Jordan. He must have heard something in those closely blended voices of Jeff, Nick, Drew and Justin to give them some of his valuable time. Whether or not 98° got his card is moot. He remembered who they were, and he got their info.

His name was Paris D'Jon.

D'Jon's D'Man!

Paris D'Jon.

Whether you remember that name now, or let it slip, doesn't make any difference, because you'll hear it again.

(Paris and his wife just had their first child! Congratulations, Paris!)

Let's go from exotic Paris, though, to Cincinnati.

Cincinnati, Ohio, that is, where three-quarters of 98° are from.

"We are all from Cincinnati, except Jeff, who is from Massillon," Justin Jeffre made clear on an AOL chat. "Drew and Nick are brothers and I went to school with them in Cincinnati and Jeff met Nick over the phone through a mutual friend. One by one we made our way out to L.A. to join the group."

One of the things that is so winning about the group of guys known as 98° is just that:

They're just guys!

Guys like you know in school, guys that hang in the mall, guys that go to your church, or guys . . .

Yeah, yeah, they dress nice now, in the latest street fashions (usually black). In fact, they have their own personal dresser. And that hair? Well, unlike Hanson, that 98° hair is certainly style to a very high degree indeed. (And doesn't Justin look good as a blond?)

Still, when they open their big mouths, what comes out is pure guy talk.

Thing is, they're nice guys, too.

Last year when asked on a Montreal TV show what their number-one wish was for, it wasn't for a number-one album. It was that world hunger should end. Their sincerity beamed through the TV waves. . . .

But where were we?

Oh, yes, Ohio!

Couldn't be a more normal state in the country than Ohio. It's got lots of beauty, lots of history, and lots of fine solid people but Ohio is certainly not the most exciting state in the country. Bedrock foundation of blue collar, salt of the earth? Sure. Scintillating? No.

Cincinnati, for instance.

Cincinnati is the world's leading manufacturer of hand tools, playing cards and soap.

And thus, from Ohio, did 98° begin with Jeff Timmons, singer.

Jeff sang in lots of bands in high school and college and he thought he'd like to make it big.

When asked on that AOL chat if any of the bands any of the group had belonged to were "garage bands," (as in a bunch of buddies banging out "Louie Louie" in a suburban basement or garage) Nick needed clarification: "Garbage, or garage?"

Justin chimed in, "We were in bands that sounded like garbage."

"We used to rehearse in our choreographer's garage," Jeff pointed out, "but we've never played in a gig in a garage. I don't know if that makes us a garage band, or not?"

Nick finished off the topic. "I don't think we ever did anything that was too terrible. We were pretty lucky that way."

Of course, they kind of led the discussion toward 98° ever being a garage band, not if individuals from the group were ever in shaggy teen bands. Maybe this is some secret skeleton in the hip and cool 98° band closet? After all they do all play instruments. Can you imagine Nick belting out "G-L-O-R-I-A" or Jeff doing hardcore punk?

We'll have to wait for the *National Enquirer* to dig up the dirt on that one.

So, he and some friends pulled up their Ohio stakes and moved to Los Angeles, which is where much of this country's music biz starts.

Of course, if Jeff had wanted to sing country-western songs, he would have moved to Nashville. Jeff didn't want to sing "Rhinestone Cowboy," though. Jeff wanted to sing "Papa was a Rolling Stone" and "Sexual Healing." Jeff had that smooth urban black sound down and he knew deep in his heart that he had a future.

He and his friends had a band and by gosh, they were going to make it in Los Angeles.

La La Land Band

Jeff's band didn't make it.

Not as the group they had started out as, anyway.

This, of course, is what often happens to bands that try to make it in L.A. For every Van Halen and Doors that roars off of Sunset Boulevard into fame and fortune, there are thousands of bands—good bands, too—that never get past FM Station or The Troubadour or The Whiskey or any of the others dozens of L.A. music nightspots.

The members of Jeff Timmons's first band had lots of obstacles to face.

Have you ever been to Los Angeles?

It's a pretty amazing place. For one thing, there's the smell of the desert and the eucaplytus there, and balmy breezes from the incredible beaches. There's traffic galore, but the temperature's pretty mild except for August and September when it gets very hot. There's great food and fascinating people. But, whew! Competition! If the people you meet sipping lattes at some Melrose coffeebar aren't in the entertainment biz, they're trying to get into the entertainment biz!

It can be very exciting in Los Angeles, but it can also be very frustrating. Unless you're independently wealthy or you're getting an allowance from Daddy in Poughkeepsie, you have to take on jobs as a waiter or temping in an office and, even then, you can't afford to live anywhere other than a cheap apartment in North Hollywood or a bad area in Los Angeles. Car insurance is expensive, rent is expensive, lifestyle is expensive—even breathing seems expensive, sometimes, in Los Angeles. (Woody Harrelson has been selling oxygen lately, for instance.)

One by one, the members of Jeff Timmons's band dropped out to pursue other goals. Or maybe just to get away from L.A.!

The only guy to remain was a guy named John Lipman.

Jeff still worked hard, and he knew that he wanted to succeed with a vocal group. He probably realized that, although he had one hot voice, and could do lead singing, he wasn't really a first lead—he needed other guys to blend with. Besides, when you're a stone fan of R-and-B groups, you want to sing with a group of other guys. You need to get that incredible *sound.* There's just nothing else like it on earth, and maybe not even in heaven!

One of Jeff's old band members was still a friend of his, and recommended that Jeff get in touch with the first thing Jeff needed for a good rhythm-and-blues group: a lead tenor!

This was none other than Nick Lachey.

Nick, though, was still in Cincinnati at this time. Jeff talked him into coming out to the coast and giving the big time a try. So Nick packed his bags and headed west.

Sure enough, Nick Lachey worked well with Jeff. Their voices blended well, they got along, they dug the same kind of music—so far so good. But still they needed more guys.

Like one bass.

One baritone!

"Hey, Jeff," Nick probably said when they were hanging out at the Sunset Tower Records, scoping out the girls and the new CDs and unable to afford either. Maybe they had Barry White on the earphones. "I know this guy back in

Cincinnati! He's not quite this rumbly deep, but you know—he's got a deep voice and he can sing like a funky bass player plays!''

Nick and Jeff got Justin's number.

Hello, Justin? How'd you like to join a group and meet gorgeous women!''

Justin shipped out quickly and sure enough, his basso was profundo. Moreover, Jeff was just as enthusiastic as the other guys about R and B, he was just as wild and crazy and fun-loving as the others, so he got along with them, and the whole adventure seemed fabulous to him.

However, there was one key part still missing.

It's called a *baritone* A baritone is a guy who can sing both high and low . . . he's kind of what they call in the music business a *midrange* singer, one who can cover certain essential notes and phrasings.

Nick Lachey, after a little time searching, most likely slapped his forehead and said, ''Hey! What about my little brother?''.

Drew could sing baritone. Moreover, he had sung with a couple of the others before.

''Well, when I was in high school,'' Drew clarifies to Exan on *YTV*, a Canadian show, ''that was the only time that we actually sang together. I was in a vocal jazz group and Nick filled in for one of the members who got ill, but other than that, he pretty much had his singing groups and I pretty much had mine, and they never really met until now.''

Drew managed to get his cute behind out to the City of Angels.

Drew was more into jazz but, then, jazz is a kissing cousin of R and B, really and if you've got the jazz swing, you can get the soul funk up pretty quick.

So they started rehearsing.

Can you just see it? Can you just conjure up in your head what it must have been like?

What was the first song they did together? ''My Girl''? A Michael Jackson song? Something by Stevie Wonder? Whew, R and B has such a vast catalog of great songs, it's hard to say. What is known, however, is that once these hot boys got going, no one could shut them up!

They'd sing everywhere they could, whether people wanted them to or not. But once people actually heard them, they generally wanted them to keep singing.

One of the strangest places was the El Toro Swap Meet in Santa Fe Springs.

"It was a kinda talent contest–swap meet," Justin explained on AOL.

"We won, but that isn't saying too much," Jeff chimed in and Drew then added: "We won a hundred dollar money tree for singing 'In The Still Of The Night,' which we still do every now and then."

Be doop a doobie doo!

Falsetto: "InnnnnthestillllovtheNieyeiiiiit!"

Great song!

So these goofy but ambitious guys were singing everywhere, but they still had to do mundane jobs to keep going, and didn't have a whole lot of money for fun.

In fact, back in those days, the evening's entertainment, once they'd stopped rehearsing, was going out and renting a 99 cent video and chomping cheap popcorn. The problem with this was that most often Jeff would fall asleep before the end of the movie and ruin everything by snoring!

However, pretty soon practice paid off, because the group just got tighter and tighter, better and better.

At this point, they called themselves Just Us. (Justin probably liked this name plenty. Certainly it was better than Jeff 'R Us.) They were also toying with changing it, and the other names they'd considered were Inertia, Next Issue, New Issue and Verse Four.

Anyway, you can just imagine Just Us (warming up to 98°) hanging around the crib. Perhaps they're a little upset about some mess that Jeff made, or they're talking about some girl that one of them just met at a Ralph's Grocery or maybe they've just finished practicing Al Green's "Take Me to the River."

Anyway, one of them has just picked up a copy of *LA*

Weekly, a free newspaper that is bursting with club and concert listings.

They're looking through it and there's the ad:

Boyz II Men!

Ooops! Time to break the piggy banks!

History beckoned!

The Audition

"Growth through harmony."

That's the motto of Boyz II Men, and the dudes of 98° must have taken that to heart, because they had all grown, musically and as people, by the time they got their first big break at that Boyz II Men show.

The smooth sounds of the group that had helped restore R and B to the forefront of American pop were probably still grooving in the ears of Jeff Timmons, Nick Lachey, Justin Jeffre and Drew Lachey as they walked into that radio station to do their stuff.

They sang and they joked and they did what they do best . . . being themselves.

In fact, they did such a great job, that none other than the illustrious Paris D'Jon called them.

Guys, he must have said. You really are determined. I like that. Plus, I like how you sound. Why not give it a shot? If you'd like me too, I'll take you under my wing.

Needless to say, the guys were thrilled.

However, for various reasons, the original baritone left the band, leaving Nick, Jeff and Justin.

They had to find themselves another baritone!

(Aside to reader: Did this occur before or after the Boyz II Men show? I've heard both from experts. We'll all just have to wait for the official 98° book to find out, alas.)

"What about Drew?" Nick most likely suggested. "My little brother! He can sing baritone!"

The guys called Drew.

Now Drew was working at the time in Brooklyn, New York. He was an emergency medical technician (a skill that came in handy during the group's journeys—more of that later).

Wanna come to California, Drew?

The fact that they had a great new manager probably helped convinced the younger guy, because he gave them a definite "Yes!"

"I quit my job, closed my bank account, packed up my car and picked Nick up at the Newark Airport and we made the three-day trek to L.A. where I learned the music to the group," Drew told *Tiger Beat*.

What was Nick doing in Newark, Drew?

Drew doesn't explain, but he does go on to state an amazing fact.

"Two days later, we opened for Montell (Jordan) at the House of Blues."

The word about the group, (now definitely called 98°, and getting hotter) had spread. They'd been doing other gigs, including opening for the Hardest Working Man in Show Business, none other than Mr. James Brown (check this guy out in the write-up on R and B later).

The reason that the boys of 98° were in Los Angeles was that record executives lived there, hung around the clubs, listened to the buzz, not just from California, but from all the music hotspots around the country, around the world.

You might think of them as a band fishing for a label.

Or, perhaps, more accurately, you might say that artists come to L.A. like schools of fish, searching for hooks to bite—hooks that were rare indeed.

In the case of 98°, though, it didn't take long for talk of the group to reach the record labels. Word was that this group was putting on some dynamic, soulful, exciting shows to warm the way for the lead act of the night, Montell Jordan, as the man toured. When that kind of word gets out, you can bet that scouts were coming to see just who the heck these white guys putting out this black harmony were!

As their manager, Paris D'Jon probably fielded lots of inquiries from record labels, he probably played it a little coy, which is normal. In this kind of business, you wait around to make sure the deal is right, and that you are getting in with the right company. A group's career has everything to do with what their record label will do for them, what contacts the publicity there has, who they'd be opening for, what radio stations they'd be played on. One of the million responsibilities of a pop group's manager is to come equipped with the knowledge and expertise—and negotiating skills—to field inquiries about a group and to spark interest.

Nonetheless, despite all the excitement 98° was sparking, all this time the boys in the band had their eyes on a single goal: Motown Records.

MOTOR CITY SOUL

"Motown" is short for "Motor Town."

Another name for "Motor Town" is "Motor City."

Motor City is, of course, Detroit, Michigan.

Detroit is the Motor City because of all the automobile factories it has. Ford, Chevrolet, Chrysler—for years they practically owned the town, and Detroit's economic woes or bliss depended entirely upon the American auto industry.

It used to be that if you said Motown, thoughts of assembly lines, the smell of hot steel, and belching factories came to mind.

Now, though, thanks to what started in the late fifties and early sixties and has kept on to the end of the millennium, when you say "Motown," people think of the record label that gave birth to such great artists as Aretha Franklin, the Temptations, the Four Tops, Marvin Gaye, the Jackson Five, Boyz II Men—and so many more, all the way up to Montell Jordan. Folks like me also think of great songs like "Heard It Through the Grapevine" and "Baby Love" and "River Deep, Mountain High," and so many more—and great songs are still coming from this fabulous record company.

Motown was started in 1958 by Berry Gordy, who had a very special idea of the kind of music he wanted the American people to hear. We'll talk some more about Motown later in the book because, if we get started now, we'll run out of room for 98°!

Anyway, anyone who's ever done cover songs (*cover* means that you're doing a song that someone else made famous!), anyone who sings R and B and soul, for that matter, does Motown songs. The guys of 98° sang a lot of them, specializing in a Temptations medley that made jaw drops.

They worshipped the artists who made this wonderful music.

This, after all, was why they'd gone to that Boyz II Men show. They wanted somehow to get the execs at Motown to know who they were!

Well, Motown knew who they were now and, thanks to canny Paris D'Jon, Motown wanted to hear the guys in person . . . but they also knew that the band was being courted by other record labels. Motown didn't just have its good name and rep to offer the boys either . . . they were now owned by the huge record company Polygram, with plenty of power and money to put behind music acts.

On April 3, 1996, the Deegs got their shot.

On that day, they not only met with Motown CEO (Chief Executive Officer) Andre Harrell, they auditioned for him.

The legend continues here for, while most bands are often asked to audition again, and there's a lot of back and forth about contracts and much negotiation that can stretch on for weeks because the record label isn't entirely sure . . .

No. In this case, a good offer was made on the spot!

Immediately, the 98° boys said Yes.

Well, after Paris D'Jon poured some cold water on them and helped them get back into their chairs after they fainted . . .

Just joshing!

Seriously, it's a fact. 98° became a Motown act on that day in April and, immediately, Motown set to work getting together the teams of people to write and produce the songs that would showcase their splendid talents.

The guys don't exactly hide the fact that they are beyond ecstasy being on Motown.

"It's such a historical legacy," Jeff told *Tiger Beat*. "Motown has had an impact on the world. If there was any label that we could have picked—it certainly was Motown."

Justin agrees.

On YTV'S *Hitlist* he said, "You know, it definitely was a dream and I don't think we really thought it would ever become reality, to be on Motown, but we got very lucky and we're very proud to say we're on Motown, the same label as Boyz II Men and Stevie Wonder and so many of our idols. I think they (Motown groups) influenced not only us, but every group that's in R&B, pop music, probably as well."

"Yeah, they shaped music to what it is today," Drew added.

One of the ironies here is that Boyz II Men were discovered at a New Edition show—(another R-and-B group), and 98° were discovered at a Boyz II Men show.

In fact, "Boyz II Men" is a New Edition song that the Philly group named themselves after.

So, is "98°" a Boyz II Men song?

No! That would be too weird, wouldn't it?

Okay. So the guys have signed their names to the dotted lines.

What's next?

Well, how about a debut album?

And what a debut!

98° in '97

Motown Records, in conjunction with their parent company, Polygram Records, released the first CD by 98° in 1997.

It's called, appropriately, *98°*.

In front of a hot red 98, the four guys looked out at you in black and white. They're sitting on a hood of an old car, and you can see the misty cityscape that could be anywhere in the urban U.S. behind them. The cover was shot in New York.

Nick's in the front, with a kind of "I'm cool! Check it out" look on that handsome face. Justin looks a little scared and Drew looks like he's thinking "I can't believe I'm on the cover of an album!"

Jeff, though, looks very happy, eager to make lots of new friends and maybe have some Skyline Chili for dinner.

It's a great picture.

The guys are all dressed in leather jackets, loose denims, plaid shirts untucked, with t-shirts keeping them warm in an all-American kind of way. They probably smell good—of English Leather cologne and Ivory soap.

They look like sharp but regular guys who are saying, Hey Girl! Wanna go for a ride? All brash and eager, but basically—well, kind of shy.

Who could resist?

Let's go take a ride!

These guys look fun and cuddly and exciting. . . . And,

hey, if they get too fresh, you don't have to punch them, just push the off button of the CD player!

Well, that's what the CD looked like. (And looks like now! Don't have it? Put down this volume, get thee to the mall and purchase!)

COME! GET IT! COME!

A warm male voice speaks, low and sexy, while a soulful guitar plunks and a synthethizer smooths funkstrings in the background. Rising up in the mix: gentle, seductive male voices, harmonizing in a pitch that touches you deep inside.

The voice welcomes you, introduces the world—and leads you into the soft and thrilling guyzone, or the mellow organization known as 98°.

Thus begins the first CD, a rousing and arousing bunch of gorgeously crafted music. Is it pop or is it R and B? It's a nice blend, like strong coffee with mild, swinging back and forth, sometimes hard and insistent, but mostly sweet and vulnerable and sexy.

"Come and Get It" is the kick-off song, and it's a good choice for the beginning of a CD. By the time the girl's voice gasps that she's accepting the invitation the singers have given, you're already there!

Still, the song that made the charts, and yanked the whole assemblage of tunes up the charts was the next one, "Invisible Man."

With its heartfelt sentiments about wanting to get someone's attention and failing, "Invisible Man" says something solid and true about tender but tearful feelings that we all go through sometimes. And it says it not just in the lyrics, but in the voices and dip and blend in emotional gyrations. Nick and Jeff show off their high but emphatically male voices well and Justin and Drew resonate and dance behind the groove with perfect tone.

Sweet!

Apparently lots of people thought so, too, because the single "Invisible Man" went gold, reaching Number 12 on the *Billboard* charts before deciding to cool it a bit before things got entirely too hot.

Although the album never made it into the top ten, and more people didn't hear it than heard it, it spun off two hit singles and videos—and it got the rest of the world very steamed up indeed!

Let's take a look at what exactly this CD was, how it was put together, by whom—and how the guys feel about the songs!

WAS IT SOMETHING THEY DIDN'T SAY?

"The album kinda covers all facets of relationships," Nick explained on an AOL chat. "Everything from the invisible man to the being in love with a girl who doesn't even care about you or know you exist, to take my breath away, where you're basically just telling a girl how wonderful she is to you and we cover everything from the joy of a relationship to the heartbreak of a relationship."

If you look at most albums, you'll see that there are generally one or two producers—mostly just one—for a CD.

In the case of the *98°* album, it might best be said that the producer for the whole album was simply Motown.

Each song has a different producer credited.

What does a producer do? Why are they important?

Well, a record producer is kind of like a movie director. He takes all the elements available and then he puts them into an imaginative and definitive mix.

For example, remember Montell Jordan? Well, he did the guys a favor in return for opening for his show so often, by producing the first song on the CD, "Come and Get It." Montel wrote it, too, so you can guess he had a definite idea of what it was supposed to sound like!

Anyway, a producer gets together the musicians. He arranges the song, and the group practices their parts.

This takes a lot of practice, and you can bet that 98° have

got the best talent in the Motown stable to help them make their records tip-top performances.

For example, in the liner notes of the group's second CD, *98° and Rising*, there is a "Coach" listed. This is George Jackson, also listed as that CD's executive producer. It's doubtful that we're talking about the guy's softball-team coach. No, Jackson must be a professional voice coach, a cosmic choir director who's purpose is help train the guys' voices and show them how to use them in absolutely the best ways.

Why did Motown sign a white R-and-B act?

The answers are both complicated and simple.

In the U.S., there are pop charts and there are R-and-B charts. It's been like this for a long time. It's part of the way music—and acts—are marketed.

Motown has for years been a part of the Polygram Company, contributing mostly to the R-and-B and hip-hop fields, but also tending their back archives and such giants as Stevie Wonder and Boyz II Men.

However, they've all been black groups.

Some articles elsewhere claim that 98° is the first white group that Motown's ever signed. This is not the case. True, it's the first white band in a long time. In the sixties and seventies, Motown tried its hand with rock (including Mynah Birds with Neil Young) and also was quite successful with Rare Earth, who did their share of R and B, but were mostly a good deal jazzier and rockier than most Motown acts. (Rare Earth still plays medium-sized halls, and still packs a punch, with a nice horn section).

However, Motown is quite aware of the world market and a phenomenon has been growing all around the world: Pop.

Well, okay—let's just say that pop got a little less—uhm—popular in the United States. Although America has got some of the most rabid music fans in the world, and its tastes are wide, the general populace of record buyers has been purchasing a great deal of alternative and country-western lately.

Oh yes, we've still been hearing from Whitney Houston

or Boyz II Men—and R and B—and hip hop and rap are large solid markets for the music companies.

But pop . . . ?

What is pop?

It's, well, whatever sells, actually, so if gansta rap was all that anyone bought—well, suddenly gangsta rap would be pop!

No, the word *pop* is sort of a catch-all, more associative than anything else. When you ask your average citizen on the street what's "pop," they might say, "Elvis" or "The Beatles" or "The Beach Boys" or "Michael Jackson" or "George Michael" or "Madonna" or . . . well, the list goes on. Even though all these pop performers come from different areas of music—Elvis Presley from rockabilly, the Beatles from R&B and rock and roll, The Beach Boys from the southern California surf sound, Michael Jackson from soul music, George Michael from British R and B, dance-pop Madonna from New York dance clubs—they all produced records and sounds that stuck stubbornly to public consciousness. This is for various reasons, but the main reasons are that the music has melody, beat, innovation and personality that jumps out from radios and grabs the listener.

When you read popular music reviews you'll hear a lot about *hooks*. Pop music must have hooks. These are melodies, harmonies, production tricks—mostly catchy parts of melodies that catch the listener's ear.

So, you've got to have a great hook, a great song, a nice beat . . . but, more than that, you've got to have great voices or a special vocal blend that can give the music that extra punch.

98° has that punch, that talent, and the packaging in their looks and smiles and personalities that go with it.

Motown saw that.

But they could see the group going different ways, and they wanted to give the guys the opportunity to be as successful as possible, which is why they tilted some of the numbers on the *98°* CD toward pop—to see if the boys would get heard more in that direction.

It was a wise decision.

THE FIRST SINGLE

Ever wonder what it's like at a radio station?

I used to.

When I was younger, I used to listen to the radio—sometimes Top 40 stations, sometimes album-oriented stations and think—wow, it must be great to be a disc jockey! You get to speak to neat people, you get to show off—and you get lots and lots of free music.

Then I worked at a radio station for a while.

For one thing, if you're a disc jockey, you don't necessarily get to choose what you play. That's done by the program director. For another, there is so much music that streams in, so many singles and albums and special promo tapes, that it's very, very hard indeed to listen to it all, much less figure out what to play.

The program director's job is to put on music that people want to hear, so the station will get a big audience and be able to charge lots for advertising. So, he or she has to keep abreast of what's happening in the music world, to know what's coming up. For this, the program director reads special trade magazines, including *Billboard*, to see what clubs are playing, to see what other stations are successful with.

Meantime, music promoters are busy trying to get the music directors' attention and convince them to play their acts' songs! Back in the late fifties, a big scandal erupted when a disc jockey/music director of an influential station was discovered to be accepting bribes to play records. This was called *payola*, and it became illegal.

So. Suppose you're Motown.

You've got a bunch of kids that do great, great versions of Temptations songs and those of other vocal bands. And they adore Boyz II Men and other R-and-B acts.

What do you do with them?

What do you have them sing on their first album?

Well, you look out at the music scene and see what's out there, but you also hedge your bets and do what you know best . . .

So, that's what happened with 98°.

But what was out there in the world of music world that was selling?

HEATING UP A COLD WORLD

Yes, Boyz II Men was a harmony group that had broken out into a huge market and, if any group was the model for 98°, it's Boyz II Men.

The problem was that other groups that had been R-and-B harmonizers—like New Kids on the Block, Color Me Badd and New Edition—had to leave the scene and head to other pastures because their style just wasn't pushing the plastic anymore.

However, vocal groups were coming back into vogue to an extent. The big news were the Spice Girls. You know, a girl group. Girl power. A manufactured group with savvy and style, personality and good PR. Lesser news in the States, but larger around the world, were Boyzone from Ireland and the various other groups that followed in that mode.

Yes, all of these groups sang pop in the simplest sense. Music with a beat, a melody, harmonizing . . . and simple, punchy hooks, aided by the latest in techonology. What was catching on as much as the production values, though, were the voice values—voices that used the vocal tricks and phrasings learned from years and years of listening to classic black singers like Otis Redding, Teddy Pendergrass, the Temptations, the Four Tops . . . the list goes on and on. These new groups were white people singing in black styles—but that's the story of rock and roll and pop. That's where this music was born. It's the well that has to be returned to for inspiration and excitement because of the deep emotional expression it holds.

One band, in particular, paid attention to what was happening around the world.

It was a boy band named the Backstreet Boys.

THE BACKSTREET CONNECTION

There's no question, in my mind, that 98° are better singers than the Backstreet Boys. Certainly they can whip the Boys' butts on *a cappella*. (And 'N Sync. Sheesh. Forgettaboutit!)

But without the Backstreet Boys, there might have been no 98°.

As noted before, the band bridles sometimes when people call them a boy band.

They certainly are much more than that, and they certainly have stronger ties with a classic form of music that will still be stirring hearts and souls long after this generation gets planted in the cutout bins.

Nonetheless, the American group that was making news in 1996 when 98° was getting record labels interested in them was a bunch of cute guys from Florida who could sing and who had personality and who the general population of the States didn't know much about—not like the rest of the world did.

The Backstreet Boys couldn't get arrested in the States at first. However, their songs—and performances—became popular first in Europe and Asia.

Only then did the kids of America start paying attention to the guys who would soon be the faves.

There's no doubt that when the producers of the first 98° album sat around a table and listened to what they had, they knew exactly what song they should release first . . . and why.

Four Very Visible Men

CD marketing is getting simple again.

Used to be, in the old days, it was the singles that mattered. You had enough singles, buyers would go off and get the album. Albums became the stars, thanks to the concept albums started by The Beatles' *Sergeant Pepper's Lonely Hearts Club Band*; singles became less and less important, but the fact remained that if you had singles that got played on the radio lots, people bought more of your albums.

Nowadays, singles are again very important. Sure, the new Whitney Houston will sell because it's Whitney Houston. But when you're a new group, you have to clock in with a hit, or you're dead.

For 98°, that necessary hit came right off the bat with "Invisible Man."

But never, never say that the guys and their manager and their company didn't work for it!

Still it's nice to know that the chemistry bettween Nick, Jeff, Justin and Drew, Paris D'Jon and Motown Records came together on this particular song.

No, it's not about the guy in the famous H. G. Wells novel or the movies based on the book.

The song is about a poor loser who can't get noticed by a girl he's nuts about. Who hasn't been in that position?

Of course, although the song is about a sad loser, in all departments it's a real winner.

Written and produced by Dane DeViller and Sean Hosein

(with a writing assist by Steve Kipner), well-known writer/ producers who've worked with such artists as The Corrs, it's a slow scorcher that sounds to me a teensy bit like the classic "Groovin' (on a Sunday Afternoon)" on the front part, and with a nice hooky middle part. All the productions are sweet, slow Motown at its best, but what really sells the song, are the vocals and their arrangements, they way they shyly slip back and forth in the melody and harmony.

Nick and Jeff sound like little lost puppies, mooning away and you can't help but fall in love with them. Justin's big, tender, voice does a speaking part and Drew does his baritone with mellow conviction.

If you wonder what it takes for a song to be a hit, just listen to this one a few times. And then try and get it out of your head!

So, the Motown guys listened to what they had and probably couldn't get it out of their heads either!

This was the first single, the one that would go out and make a stab at the charts and prepare the way for the coming of the album.

But, in the age of MTV, there's a little something extra you need to get your song listened.

You gotta have a video!

So the guy went and did the "Invisible Man" video.

THE STUFF OF MTV

When you listen to the first album by 98°, you have to say, wow! Motown spared no expense in putting the best on this CD!

So much so that they must have been short of cash when it came around to doing the video for "Invisible Man."

They shot it quickly on Long Island, New York.

Yes. That's about it.

It's the guys singing in a warehouse. Black and white.

It's the guys singing in the rain. Black and white.

Of course, inexpensive doesn't mean bad. The photography is great, the performances are fine.

And the black and white is actually a master stroke, a continuation (or lead-up to, come to think of it) the monochrome photos that distinguish the album.

Black and white is great to show off male good looks to good effect, and the guy's strong features and clean-cut handsomeness come off sharp as male models for a clothing line. Plus, they look winsome, sad and tuneful. Just like the song.

The single was released.

The video was launched.

However, the group and their label had to do more than just sit back and rest on their laurels.

No, in fact, the really hard work was just beginning.

PROMO, MOE!

Thanks to the brilliant work of their manager, Paris D'Jon, the boys had already been doing plenty of shows, getting their name out. This, in clubs and as warmups for better known groups.

However, now that they had a single out, and an album coming up, they had to get out and sing and let people know what a great group they were.

This is where a manager and label come in handy. Meetings are held, strategies are formed. Of course, in such a situation, there is one principle way of getting noticed—tried and true!

Tour, young men!

The guys hit the road, travelling all over the U.S.A, Canada, England, Germany, and Asia.

They did all kinds of shows, from night clubs to regular concerts to signings at record stores.

Fortunately, people starting to take notice of "Invisible Man," and the single started climbing the charts.

The full album came out, complete with all its goodies,

and a righteous album it was, full of good stuff. With writers and producers as talented at Montell Jordan, Dane Deviller, Sean Hosein, Mario Winans and Tricky and Sean, all under the eagle eye of the maestros of Motown, how could it be anything but!

Even the guys got into the act, writing and producing my personal favorite on the CD, "Completely," with Bernard Grubman, and then doing an amazing job with a sweet, sweet *a cappella* version.

However, even great records don't always sell well.

And, although some pop bubbles up on *98°*, at its heart it's pure, pure, excellent R and B. Some critics claimed that it sounded like any other R and B. Why did you need some white guys doing this stuff, when you had groups like Boyz II Men and others already? Perhaps the feeling in the R-and-B circles was that while it was nice that the guys were singing well, they weren't doing anything innovative or new with the material.

In fact, that's not the case at all, and we'll discuss that later when we look at the CDs closer.

That the two CDs are different, no one can dispute. Clearly, when Motown signed the group they did have the idea of giving these guys a pop shot, but they hedged their bets by making the record pure and basic R and B. From Justin Jeffre's Barry White imitation that kicks it off, to "I Wanna Love You," the first CD is a catalog of modern R-and-B style.

It's hard to tell what the thinking was with the first CD. However, as soon as "Invisible Man" started making a little noise on the pop charts, and the analysts realized where it was getting attention, the opportunity was grabbed.

These guys maybe were following in the footsteps of R-and-B greats, true. The hearts they were winning, though, were the same hearts that had already been wooed and won by others.

But they were big hearts . . .

And they had plenty of room for lots of good music.

BAND ON THE RUN

There's absolutely no record of this, but I would think that at sometime around the time that Paris D'Jon took on the group he must have sat Jeff Timmons, Nick Lachey, Justin Jeffre and Drew Lachey down and said something like this:

"Guys, you have talent. There's a lot of talent out there, though. What impressed me besides the talent, though, was your determination. The work you've been doing. All this talent contest stuff . . . the sheer willpower and doggedness it took to do the anthem for that baseball game . . . And the way you tried to get to see Boyz II Men by singing . . . Impressive. But when you did that radio gig, I realized you guys might just have what it takes.

"Yes, you're good looking. Yes, you can sing. Yes, you have good personalities and are nice guys. But, without something vital here, you're not going to make it in this business. That's very hard work. And that means willingness to roll with the punches, to take defeat in stride and head off for the next gig. Not all your records may make a dent. This was never an easy business and it's even harder now.

"Most of all you have to believe in the music, in yourselves and in making a difference in the world. A difference that might help people. Because that's all that really matters."

Obviously, the guys were up to it.

You have to wonder sometimes if they fully knew what they were getting into!

I've read plenty of interviews and talked to musicians about what it's like. On the surface the life seems glamorous and all fun—but think about it, really and truly.

Life on the road is tough.

Some bands are stuck travelling around in a van and crashing on people's sofas or staying in cheap hotels. However, as soon as 98° and single "Invisible Man" started getting lots of airplay and their label wanted them to go out on the road the band got a tour bus, so they had a place they could sleep every night and still hit a lot of gigs.

In their interview with Exan on YTV in Canada, the attractive presenter actually goes up to the bus (or is it an RV?—you can't quite tell) and knocks on the door. And the affable foursome alight to be charming and cute and sing a little bit.

With a schedule like theirs, they probably were inside their home away from home, trying to catch forty winks!

Shows and radio stations and record stores, shows and radio stations and record stores. Interviews, singing, interviews, singing . . . The guys were just nonstop.

The science of marketing is pretty exact these days, and it didn't take long for Motown to realize who was buying the single and who liked the CD the most.

Yes, teenage girls.

But there were probably lots of teenage girls who either hadn't heard of four lovable heart-throbs,—or even if they'd heard "Invisible Man," didn't know what matinee idols 98° were.

How could the band reach these potential fans?

Well, nowadays, they could appear on *Dawson's Creek* or something like that. Even so, that wouldn't give the full impact of the live, smiling, harmonizing quartet.

No. Live shows were the ticket.

But where?

And here was where a genius had a brilliant idea that would help 98° really get rolling as a boy band, whether they liked that appellation or not!

TEEN SCREAMS

There's an infamous movie from the sixties, a baddie called *Where the Boys Are.*

If you were to make a quickie about the 98° start-up career, you might call it *Where the Girls Are.*

So, where are the girls? Well, malls, yeah. Schools would

be good, but schools are pretty localized and there are so, so many. Besides, there are only so many dances and junior proms, and most halls of education frown on record companies sending in studs to distract female students.

However, remember that the CD *98°* and the single "Invisible Man" were released in the spring and getting listened to on summer vacation.

Where, oh where . . . ?

Someone at Motown must have gotten a big raise later, because someone came up with a brainstorm.

Cheerleader camps!

That's where lots and lots of teenage girls were.

This stroke of total genius worked extremely well!

Under the guidance of Paris D'Jon, the guys started doing gigs at cheerleading camps. Why was this brilliant?

Well, not just because teenaged females could witness the virile and blazing brilliance that is 98° in full-throated action. These camps have attendees from lots of different places. 98° could preach to them the 98° word, and then the girls, after camp, could disperse to spread the 98° gospel.

And those shows were something else indeed!

"You can't lose if you're going to a cheerleader camp," Jeff told *Popstar* magazine. "You can basically sing 'e-i-e-i-o.' It was a good confidence-builder to get us comfortable. We did that for a month or two. It was crazy. Some of those girls were 13 or 14 years old, but they were so fanatical they pushed the stage we were on back a few feet!"

Imagine! You've been prancing around all day, doing sis-boom-bahs and what have you. You haven't seen any guys for weeks, and into your midst come four gorgeous dream-boats to serenade you!

98° must have indeed been a religious experience for many girls that summer.

And, when the girls got back to school after Labor Day, you can bet they were cheering more than the football team!

THE GREAT BIG WORLD

"Invisible Man" reached as high as twelve on the charts, and lingered for quite a few weeks.

The folks at Motown, though, knew that there was a great big world out there. In Britain, Europe and Asia, the Queens were the Spice Girls and the Kings were the Backstreet Boys.

"Invisible Man" was making news overseas, too, and while the album wasn't quite making record sellers as happy as the Spice Girls and Backstreet Boys were, it was holding its own.

The strategy was obvious.

Send the guys over to conquer the old country!

Again, you have to remember that pop music is big news around the world. It never went away. And avid pop fans are always eager to enjoy fresh young talent.

Again, brilliant strategy and hard, hard work came into play. 98° did the tour and interview thing.

On one trip to Europe they were lucky enough to be seated right next to the Backstreet Boys at the MTV Europe awards. Every little exposure was a boon, and it turned out that the Boys and the Guys got on great.

In England, where R and B is quite the rave and where pop stars seem to spring up like crumpets at a tea party, career engineers Paris D'Jon and the Polygram/Motown wizards got our guys hooked up with an exciting British phenomenon: The Smash Hits tour.

This tour is actually an annual junket that cruises from city to city in Great Britain and shows off fresh young talent for the pop trade. The bands do their stuff, the potential fans get an eyeful—and everyone gets a chance to party and play and laugh and hear some good music.

Now, you have to understand something here. While 98° fans (and perhaps even to a great degree, Backstreet Boy aficionados and 'N Sync nuts) are big music lovers, its a little bit different over in Britain.

The Brits are loony about pop music. They are obsessed. Pop music is vital in young British life. There are, at last count, two weekly music newspapers for the public (*New Music Express* and *Melody Maker*) and another regular journal (*Smash Hits*, natch) and all one of the five major national radio bands (BBC1) does is to play pop.

The Brits also love American music, so the British Isles are an important market for American acts. (Did you know, for instance, that one of the most popular forms of music on Irish radio is good ol' American country-western?) However, the first thing you realize when you listen to Brit pop acts as opposed to most American pop acts is how much more polished they are. (Why is this? Me, I think it's because they're more intense and they practice more.)

It's America, after all, where the term *garage band* comes from. Lots of American music is loose and fun, but sometimes kind of sloppy. This is of course part of its tradition, but still, tight and well-rehearsed music, including pop or R and B, can be some of the most exciting to listen to, particularly live.

In short, the bar is a little higher in Britain.

And on the Smash Hits tour, 98° would have to rest more on their tight harmonies and their tight—er—dimples.

In 1997, 98° did the Smash Hits tour with Five, All Saints, and a few other new bands.

Well, 98° showed everyone they were more than just pretty faces, winning over their audiences with their fine style and class.

Although the did not win the Best Band award (that was Five—another pop group to watch out for, definitely) their presense and performance in Britain was rewarded by many new fans.

Something happened, though, in Britain that was not so great—but showed what great character and what pros the guys of the group truly are.

Low Point, High Point

THAT CLUB IN LEEDS

Like I said, the band worked hard.

One of the things that helps when you're a young pop group, you've got the energy for touring. However, it takes more than energy to deal with rough things that happen.

While in Britain, the band was booked to play in a club in a northern industrial town. Good idea, because Britain industrial towns, like Manchester and Sheffield and others, are musical hotbeds.

Alas, someone didn't look at a calendar when they booked 98° in Leeds.

"I think it was this place in England. Leeds, wasn't it?" The interview was for *Galaxie* magazine, and the other guys nodded, Yes, it was Leeds. "Well, they scheduled us to do this appearance in a club on Guy Fawkes Day, which is one of their national holidays, so everybody's out watching fireworks and roasting marshmallows or something like that. The club was so tiny, and there was hardly anyone there. There was half a dozen people in there, seven people at most, and they had us performing on the floor, and the sound system was a disaster. The whole thing was a disaster, but we still managed to put on a show to the best of our ability. But it was probably one of the low points of our career."

So the guys put on a great show for that tiny audience like the troopers they are.

"We really would go on for one person if we had to," Nick said in the interview. "Honestly, we feel like everybody counts." They took the experience and moved on. Instead of being bitter and disappointed, they realized this what they'd signed up for, this kind of disappointment.

But they proved that whether you're in a audience of six or six thousand, when you're at a 98° show, you're in for one heck of a great show.

They also enjoyed their experience in Britain very much, despite the heavy-duty competition they must have faced from that incredible line-up that was with them. (More about All Saints and Five in particular later, if you haven't heard about these groups, you really should.)

The guys thought that Five were super.

But they were particularly taken with All Saints. (A bunch of beautiful girls—no wonder!)

Clearly, if the guys had their druthers, this is the band that they'd have open for them on any upcoming tour they wanted to!

However, of all the places that the guys toured, it should be mentioned that the places where they made the biggest initial impact were the most exotic.

Almost Too Hot for 98°

While the follow-up to the hit single "Invisible Man" "Was It Something I Didn't Say," was not quite as big a hit in the States as that first catchy smash, "Something" showed strong results in Asia, and already signals were coming that 98° was getting extremely popular in various Far East countries.

Why Asia?

That's probably a question mostly Americans ask. For American pop fans, the world is bordered by Los Angeles and New York, with the British Isles an orbiting satellite that sends down bands from time to time.

In fact, the whole world is crazy about pop. Although every country has its own native music, for some reason, per-

haps because communications got better in the twentieth century, the popular music of America and Great Britain and the
rest of Europe spread all over the globe. Why? Well, you
have to remember that the British Empire of the nineteenth
century spread British culture, British people and the English
language everywhere. Although there were many significant
clashes with native peoples, the Brits were more interested in
enlightening (and making money from) the people they col-
onized. As a result, many, many different kinds of peoples
are as familiar with the Beatles as with Beethoven.

Oh. Also, pop music is fun.

You only have to go to Japan to see the impact of Western
pop music. Many Japanese musicians emulate pop styles generally abandoned by Western musicians today. You only have
to watch a few of the growingly popular Japanese *anime*—
Japanese cartoons—to hear echoes of the fifties and early
sixties American Top 40. (In this case, the Japanese probably
heard that brand of music from the many American soldiers
based in that country after World War II.)

This is also the case in the Philippines.

A thorough study should be made of all this, of course—
but it's a fact that the precursors of 98°—the Backstreet Boys,
of course—became very popular in the Philippines.

Again, there are many ties between the Philippines and
America—ties that go back beyond World War II to the
American imperialist days of President Theodore Roosevelt.
Although the Philippine Islands are not owned by the U.S.,
most Filipinos certainly know the difference between the
Beach Boys and 'N Sync!

Don't pin me down on this, but I don't think that modern R
and B has been that popular in Asia in the past. However,
the work of pop artists like the Bee Gees, George Michael,
Tina Turner and Whitney Houston has prepared the way for
the more concentrated dosage. For some reason, although this
stuff—from hip hop to rap and funk—is hardcore black music, created and done best by black American artists, Asian
pop fans seem to prefer it in slightly altered form from white

British or American artists. We'll leave the explanation for this to sociologists, but merely point out irrefutable evidence.

Thousands of screaming girls.

The Asian girls seem to adore Backstreet Boys, 'N Sync and the Brit groups like Boyzone, Take That and Five, not just because they are cute guys—for some reason, this very emotional and deep music created in a deep pool of tradition, social injustice, love, fear and frustration, anger and joy connects with them.

In any case, they love it.

And 98° were more than happy to take their music—and their smiles and clean-cut personalities—overseas to show them.

THE FIRST ASIAN TOUR

So, in March '98, the band went to the fans.

It was part promotional tour, part concert tour—and all very, very hot.

In fact, the guys were sweating like crazy.

While our hemisphere is just letting go of the shivers in March, down in the Southern Far East, it's still very much summer.

This was to be the first of three visits in 1998 for 98°.

During a talk with *Lime* magazine, on a later trip, the interviewer pointed out that they'd come at a time when many of their fans were busy with exams and really couldn't give the group the attention they deserved.

"Yeah," Drew said, "But our fans have been so great! We flew in at midnight and there were so many fans at the airport with cards and presents. We were really touched! But our most memorable experience has to be in Malaysia during our first visit in March. We didn't really know what to expect and were very excited when we realized we had so many fans there."

During an interview for the Asian magazine *Teens*, the guys were asked how Asian fans were different. One of them responded: "In America, the fans come up to you and you know they wanna scream, but they are like 'I'm too cool for that.' But here in Asia, they just do it. The fans in Indonesia were the craziest. They would hide behind laundry baskets in the hotel."

Drew went on, "Yeah, the fans would hide at the fire escapes in the hotel and when they would hear our voices, they'd jump out at us."

The interviewer asked if that was scary.

Nick laughed. "Nah. There's nothing scary about teenage girls."

Fans galore indeed. In the Philippines, they got plenty of welcome receptions as they did radio interviews and club dates.

The impact of the visit still lingers. On one of the many websites that sprang up as monuments to love for 98°, a fan wrote about her experience actually interacting with the guys. Apparently, she got a press pass and was permitted to take pictures. The result was a telling commentary on what the guys are like during one of these junkets.

The fan was thrilled when, during a recording date, the guys were so hot they had to take off their shirts. (Apparently, much of the Asian female response to 98° is because they're so buff and are happy to show it.) But what impressed her the most was how honestly thrilled the group seemed to be about being in Manila and getting a good response to their music. She found them enthusiastic and fun to talk to on a personal level.

Poor Nick had a bad stomachache, so he had to rest some.

Poor Jeff had to opt out of some interviews because he was having voice problems, and had to rest his golden pipes for singing.

When they left, the fan was only too happy to report that these guys were exactly what we've said they were—nice guys, absolutely thrilled to be doing what they were doing. (In fact, at the end of the trip, when the hotel was thronged by fans, Justin was upset that they had to leave via the back way to avoid the riot of excitement their music and muscles had stirred up. He wanted to say goodbye!)

Similar stops occurred throughout Asia, to similar effect.

Although their album was quite popular, it was their two singles that had initially gotten these folks stirred up.

The first, of course, was "Invisible Man," a song that became popular enough that Motown decided to do another video for it. Thus, there are actually two videos of "Invisible Man." The second has the guys interacting with beautiful women, which they probably enjoyed a great deal, knowing them. This was probably the video that got most play in Asia before their tour.

However, their second single—the one that didn't get quite the attention "Invisible Man" got—also had a video which probably got them attention in Asia.

Was It Something I Didn't Play?

There seems something prophetic in the naming of this band.

Not only is the music warm and feverish, not only are the guys what their fans term *hotties*, but, quite often, the guys of 98° get themselves into places that are, well, hot!

Of course, when in concert girls don't mind much when they take off their tops and ripple those muscles. Sometimes, though, it's just plain uncomfortably hot.

According to an article in *Teen People* about the making of the video for the *98°* video "Was it Something I Didn't Say" the guys worked up a big sweat, dancing for the hours and hours it took to make the video. "My shirt smells like death," said Jeff, sniffing a pit. Dripping perspiration, Nick put in: "We might be exceeding ninety-eight degrees."

As you may recall, the song itself bemoans the loss of a girlfriend because the singer neglected to say he loved her. Real stupid, yes, but, unfortunately, very common, it would seem.

*   *   *

The director of the video, Darren Grant, who's done lots of hit R-and-B videos for people like Brian McKnight, came up with the idea of giving each of the guy's an "ex-girlfriend" for the video, then having the guys lost in a dark maze without the girls.

The video went out and the song did *some* business. The album did well enough for Motown to realize that they had something here.

And they certainly couldn't complain about the numbers of teenaged girls who started falling in love with these handsome, clean-cut guys and their rich and full harmonies.

Nor could they complain about the hard work and commitment of Nick, Jeff, Drew and Justin.

"Music is my life," Jeff has said, and music—and the dedication of the fans that the group had picked up along the way—kept them going through the occasional rough spots that every starting group faces. This band is tenacious.

When Jeff had to lip synch his solo parts for the "Was It Something I Didn't Say?" video, he had to do it over and over and over again. Each time, he put in a heartfelt performance, and it just kept on getting better and better.

How did he keep this up? he was asked.

"It's about feeling the music and listening to the lyrics," he answered.

Obviously, that's what the group has been doing all along, and it's what's keeping them going.

Let Me Take You Higher

For Jeff Timmons, Drew Lachey, Justin Jeffre and Nick Lachey, 1997 was a pretty amazing year.

But for 98°, '98 was even better.

That first incredible Asian tour was in March '98, and life just improved.

The guys already knew what was going to happen when they got home, and they were only too happy to tell Asian journalists all about the fact that they were going to be working on their next single with a very special artist indeed. But the experience itself was even better than they'd anticipated.

GETTING WEAVY WITH STEVIE

Ever since Disney Feature Animation starting getting R-and-B artists involved with singing on soundtracks to their features (like *Beauty and the Beast* they've made sure that they had at least one song tacked onto the project that would be emblematic of the spirit of the project, and could also serve as the basis for a video to get MTV and VH-1 play.

Upcoming on the animation schedule was an exciting movie called *Mulan*, the story of a Chinese woman way back in history who masqueraded as a male warrior and defeated a Mongol invasion of her country.

Exactly how does R and B fit into a Chinese motif? Well, actually, the Disney think tank was already halfway there, getting the incredible talent of Eddie Murphy to play Mulan's cute dragon companion with his full ethnic arsenal.

However, they still needed a pop single.

What came up was a song called "True to your Heart" a piece of pop glory that just begged for a hot harmonica part.

And nobody but nobody has a more recognizable harmonica attack than Stevie Wonder, he of soul legend. The blind but visionary artist had been a part of Motown's stable since the early sixties, first as "Little Stevie" Wonder. But just as soon as he got more control of his music, he trailblazed with some great albums (oops . . . check out the little section on Stevie included in this book).

Stevie Wonder has said that at first he was hired to do the project for just the harmonica, and then was asked to sing too. At the risk of being wrong, I'd like to conjecture as to how 98° got into this act.

Okay, so Motown knows that its guy, Stevie W., was going to do what looked to be a hit. So, maybe they said, Hey Disney folk! How about this! We've got this hot new singing group that would be perfect for this song. We'd like to pair them with Stevie and get them more exposure.

All the Mickey Mouse folk had to so was to listen to that first CD to realize that these boys had the goods to deliver a terrific performance. So, they must have grabbed the chance.

It worked well, even though they weren't in the studio at the same time.

98° were in Asia. Stevie Wonder was doing concerts in Asia.

Thanks to the wonder of technology, though, it sounds as though they were in the same studio having one heck of a good time.

"It was a real thrill and the highlight of our career," Justin told a Disnel Channel chat.

"It was a great thrill to work with both Disney and Stevie Wonder and to be a part of such a historic production."

The studio work was only part of the process. The guys also had to make a video, which featured them and Stevie involved in whimsical intrigue in New York's Chinatown, intercut, of course, with clips from the movie.

It was also the first time they actually *met* Stevie.

"For the video," Drew also told the questioners at the Disney Chat, "it was great to be working with Stevie. He was cracking jokes and (he) made us feel very comfortable."

Certainly on their momentous first visit to *The Tonight Show* along with the Motown legend, Stevie was cracking jokes.

ONWARD AND UPWARD

In June 1998, when 98° appeared with Stevie Wonder on *The Tonight Show*, it was yet another high point in their lives.

"Millions and millions saw us on it!" Nick enthused to *Lime* magazine about that momentous occasion.

With Stevie Wonder behind his keyboards, his dreadlocks hanging down and his smile way up high and the crack *Tonight Show* band behind them, 98° had never done a better job on the air than here, delivering a strong and stirring, and obviously live version of the song. (All too often, singing groups don't even sing their songs when on TV. Because of production limitations, they have the microphones turned off, and then lip synch. But then, this sort of thing is pretty obvious when it happens. Generally, if the song sounds *just* like the record, it probably *is* the record!)

After a commercial break, Stevie took his place by Jay Leno, the guys looking very happy to be placed around them.

Jay said something like "Hey, Stevie—did you know these guys aren't black?"

Stevie tilted down his trademark sunglasses and pretended to look at Nick, Jeff, Drew and Justin closely. "Oh dear!" he said, or something like that. Everyone laughed.

Alas, none of the members of 98° had a chance to say anything! Stevie and Jay yakked away, but no one asked 98° anything. This didn't seem to bother the guys though. They were grinning much too much for that.

THE SECOND ALBUM

The guys did some work on promoting the song with appearances hither and thither, but most of their work around the time they appeared on *The Tonight Show* was probably on their new CD, *98° and Rising*.

If you'll check out the sections here on both the albums, you'll notice a rather startling fact: different producers used for the different songs (generally in the past—and now, come to think of it—most records are helmed by a single producer). In these days of the resurgence of R and B and pop, this does not seem to necessarily be the case.

You'll see, for instance, that although they live in New York, the guys not only record in different studios around the New York area—they record their songs in different places around the world.

"True to Your Heart," for instance, was recorded in Los Angeles. The other songs have their beginnings in places like Vancouver, B.C., Georgia—even Stockholm! Now, it's certain that the guys have spent time in Vancouver. They've called it one of their favorite cities. But Stockholm? Did they fly there during their European tour to record there? There's no other credit for vocals, so they must have gone to Scandinavia.

With all this jetting about, Jeff, Nick, Justin and Drew must have plenty of frequent-flyer miles now!

In any case, the CD was completed in summer and fall of 1998, and slated for release October 27, 1998. After careful thought and testing (and probably listening closely to the response of audiences at shows) the next single was selected. This, of course, was "Because of You."

Alas, there wasn't a whole lot of time to rest after the final studio touches were put on *98° and Rising*.

*   *   *

In the high-pressure world of today's music business you simply can't make a hit song without a video. This, of course, is because many kids get much of their music listening done in front of the family entertainment center, watching MTV.

For "Because of You," the director had a few interesting ideas. The result is probably the best video for 98° yet. It has them singing in a summer field, which looks safe and relaxing. But, then, midsong, they're suddenly on the top of the Golden Gate Bridge by San Francisco.

It's a pretty breathtaking sight, as a helicopter swoops past showing just how high they are, and what a panoramic view of the city!

And, if you look closely, while the other guys are all making expansive hand gestures, Jeff is holding on fast to the fence, trying his best to look totally cool.

HOPPING AROUND THE WORLD

By now, the strongholds of 98° support had been pretty much established.

As with many pop sensations, the United States had generally lagged behind in appreciation of 98°. It took a long time, for instance, for the States to appreciate the pop phenomenon that was the Backstreet Boys, a bunch of guys from Florida, for goodness sake! While they were doing massive shows in Europe and Asia, nobody recognized them back home. This has changed. The truth is probably that other places are a little more in tune with new cultural things occurring, while the bulk of the American audience aren't even aware of things happening in parts of their own country!

After a little bit of downtime to rest up, see their families and enjoy some recreation, 98° had to head off to start promoting their new single and album . . . the start of a long, long haul to make sure that everyone knew it was out there.

For this reason, they hit their strongholds first.

For the third time in 1998, the guys, under the skillful guidance of Paris D'Jon headed off for Asia, with stopovers in the Philippines, Thailand, Singapore and Malaysia, just like before.

Another 98° stronghold is Canada, particularly the Toronto and Montreal areas. Here they did a number of shows and interviews, and generally pushed "Because of You."

Afterward, they headed back to Europe.

England has been jealous of its own particular pop phenoms, such as Boyzone and Take That and Five—and thus has been a harder nut to crack for the guys. However, Germany and other European countries are huge fans—particularly after the Ninety Eighters appeared on the European MTV awards.

While in Europe, the guys also sang "True to your Heart" a lot to promote the opening of *Mulan* in Europe. They were a particular hit in Europe's version of Disney World, outside Paris.

"(When we go to) Germany, there will be four to five hundred girls waiting at the aiport," Paris D'Jon predicted in *Teen People*. "And we can't go to Canada without notifying the police and telling them we're coming, because it's total madness."

That's pretty much what happened on this leg of the tour.

Significantly, the guys used the time to make a few changes.

Drew, Nick and Jeff—particularly Jeff—had pumped up more. Justin, presumably was staying out too late partying to hit the weight room quite as much, but his was the most radical change: He had his hair done totally.

And he looked good, too!

Many, many interviewers and others commented positively on the new do on this trip. However, not to be outdone, the others had a few hair changes done as well, with Nick getting a few blond lights, and the others getting subtle streaks.

No one has dreadlocks yet or is wearing goggles. The basic look of the band is still clean-cut American. But why not have some fun?

If anything, the new do perked the guys up even more, because all their appearances promoting the new single and album were absolutely ebullient.

They appeared on a request show on MTV, totally charming the audience of young girls. Overlooking New York's famous Times Square, they did some terrific *a cappella* versions of their songs, including, by request, their knockout version of ''She's Out of My Life'' which melted a large part of the audience into adoring puddles.

Another example of the guys' charm and glow shined forth at Macy's Thanksgiving Parade. It was raining and cold. Still, the sun was shining and it was a warm 98° on the Mr. Peanut float as 98° waved to everyone, and then stopped to lip synch ''Because of You.''

By Thanksgiving, they had plenty to be happy about. Although the CD itself was hanging around at the bottom half of the Billboard Hot 100, it was slowly inching its way up. And ''Because of You'' had hit the Top 10 Singles Chart—while it wobbled back and forth between five and six it evidently had taken extra pitons and dug into that steep slope for the long haul.

Next, the guys did a nice turn on a daytime show in a nicely directed turn at ''Because of You.'' Again, they didn't get to talk much.

In December, they did a number of promotional shows on radio stations, with stops all over the east coast, including Washington D.C. and Baltimore.

December 7 was a red-letter day for the group, though, as they took some time out from touring and had a special celebration at New York hot spot The Motown Cafe to accept two special awards.

One was a platinum record to celebrate ''Because of You'' selling one million copies.

The other was a gold record to celebrate *98° and Rising* selling five hundred thousand copies.

Not bad, for an album that had been out only a little over a month.

However, there was a heck of a lot more work to be done.

Along with full concerts in places like New York and Toronto, the guys also played charity gigs like the Jingle Ball in New York, and popped up at a NFL football game or two, singing the national anthem *a cappella*.

They did a Ricki Lake show, and sang with Donnie Osmond on the *New Donnie and Marie show* on New Year's Eve. They were also awarded a gold record for their work on the *Mulan* soundtrack on the show.

It was a jubilant and thrilled 98° that appeared on the MTV New Year's Eve Bash with their friend Jennifer Love Hewitt. The strange thing is that they didn't look a tiny bit tired from the most grueling year of their lives.

Sure, their CD had gone gold in a few countries. Sure, "Because of You" was stubbornly entrenched in the Billboard Top Ten Charts. Although they got mobbed in Canada, Germany and Asian countries, in their own country lots of people didn't even know who they were yet. *Time* magazine had just lumped them together with Backstreet Boys and 'N Sync, not only as a boy band but as one of the worse phenomena of 1998. Worse, they hadn't gotten anywhere near as popular as those other guys.

Boo hoo?

No way.

"We're blessed."

That's the quote you read over and over again in interview after interview. These guys love music, they love life, they love people . . . and they're grateful for getting the chance to share, to entertain, and to have fun along the way. They're giving back, too. Even before they were signed, they were using the talents for charitable purposes.

But wait . . .

Jeff, Nick, Drew and Justin weren't all smiles just because of all that.

Nope. They knew they had a great year ahead of them. They knew they'd be appearing on the Howie Mandel show soon. They knew they'd have the honor of opening for Dru Hill on their upcoming tour of Europe.

98° knew that, at the end of February, their next radio

single would be "The Hardest Thing," a wonderful song that was voted for by thousands of 98° fans—and for people to own that song, they'd have to buy *98° and Rising*, keeping it on the charts longer.

They also knew that there were at least three other songs on the CD good enough to be radio singles. They knew they had a breakthrough tour coming up in March and April. A tour on which they were not only the lead attraction, but a tour on which they'd be able to play a full hour-plus show, with a hot Motown backing band.

As they laughed and played with Jennifer Love Hewitt that night, you can almost see them thinking, Oh man! You think *1998* was the year of 98°.

In 1999, things will be even hotter.

So hot, maybe, in 1999 the group will have to change their name.

Would you believe: 99°?

First Degree: Jeff Timmons

Did you know what started Jeff Timmons singing? Church choir? Nope. School choir? Nope. Disney movies? Nope. Showers? Nope.

Girls!

That's right. Jeff told *Pop Star* magazine:

"I was a junior (in college) and met up with some guys, and some girls asked us to sing for them—so we started singing and I kind of thought it sounded good."

Jeff must have hummed a few bars before. Still, this incident must have made him realize two important things:

1. His voice sounded best in a group.
2. Girls paid attention to him when he sang in a group!

Jeff's full name is Jeffrey Brandon Timmons.

He was born on April 30, 1973 to James and Trish Timmons, in Canton, Ohio. The Timmons family already had a son, Michael, when Jeff was born, and they went on to produce a girl name Kristina after Jeff.

Jeff is the only member of 98° who wasn't born in Cincinnati. Still, he's definitely an Ohioan, raised in Massillon, Ohio.

"(Massillon) is a small town in Northern Ohio," he told *Lime* magazine. "It's a blue collar town with a population of only about 40,000. Folks there are nice and polite."

Jeff's parents divorced awhile back, but that doesn't seem to have hurt his view of relationships. He remains close to them both, visiting his father in Ohio and his mother and stepfather in Orange County, California as often as possible.

Jeff had a very normal upbringing in Massillon. He played football and dreamed of a career with the pros. He also learned to play the trombone and harmonica. Playful and high-spirited, Jeff was a typical teenager.

"I remember skipping school," he told *Teens* magazine. "My girlfriend had a car and there was once that I cut school and I was driving her car in the afternoon. I stopped at a traffic light and my mom pulled up next to me, so she caught me!"

A good-looking jock, he went off to college at Penn State University in Pennsylvania, where he majored in psychology. Although he dreamed of football, he had more realistic goals in mind.

"Besides football," he told *Popstar*, "I wanted to work with kids in some way, like being a pediatrician or child psychologist."

He actually didn't start singing seriously until one day he and a bunch of friends were clowning around and decided to put on an impromptu show for some girls. He was twenty years old.

The girls they were trying to impress were so wowed, they shrieked with pleasure. "You have a very nice voice," one of the girls told Jeff. "You ought to consider becoming a professional!"

Stars in his eyes, Jeff decided to do just that.

Shortly after this formative incident, Jeff decided, along with a group of pals, to really have a go at becoming singing stars. As a group called Just Us, they packed up and headed for the capital of American recorded music, Los Angeles, California.

Success did not come soon.

Although Jeff got some acting jobs in commercials, and he and the others in the group sang at shows, talent nights and contests, they had to support themselves in various other ways. Jeff was big and strong enough, for instance, to get security jobs at L.A. nightclubs.

Jeff was also the most dedicated of the guys who came out to make it in L.A. Years without any success had its toll. One by one, the others dropped out.

Jeff wasn't about to give up, though. He wanted to soldier on—and he didn't think that he could do it alone. No, he knew somehow instinctively that he needed other guys to sing with, to make that magic.

He got in touch with Nick—and then with Jeff and Drew—to sing in his group, Just Us. Meanwhile he was busy practicing the musical instrument he plays, the harmonica.

Success still was a bit stubborn. The guys played all over, singing wherever they could.

But then, in 1996, Jeff's idols, Boyz II Men, were playing in L.A. He'd heard about how encouraged Nick had been by the group Take 6—about how you just had to keep on persevering. But he was just as impressed that Nick had gotten backstage to talk to the famous *a cappella* group.

So, why not try that with Boyz II Men! Maybe they could sing for them and any record company people hanging out, and get a break!

That break came, and the full story is in the book, in the Legend of the Band section.

Suffice it to say, though, that it was Jeff's spirit and determination that gave 98° its drive and ambition. Talent, too, of course—

And the desire to sing to girls!

Since they've been successful, Jeff spends as much free time as possible with his family. He's dated lots of girls but finds it difficult keeping a relationship going while on the road touring and recording so much.

The rumor mills have connected him romantically with such famous women as Jennifer Love Hewitt and Mariah Carey. Research, however, has shown that *romance* is not the precise word.

Jeff definitely knows Jennifer Love Hewitt, but they're friends, nothing more.

They don't see each other much anymore due to their busy schedules (although they got to hang out recently at the MTV

New Year's Bash that Love hosted), but they do speak on the phone from time to time.

"I remember talking to her when she was shooting that movie (*I Still Know What You Did Last Summer*)," Jeff told *Teen Celebrity* magazine. "And she wasn't too thrilled about all the tight outfits and everything. But with all the pressures of being in a movie, what do you do?"

As for Mariah Carey, that one's been going around for a while.

"I read the story about her asking me out," he told *Max* magazine. "All I can say is I wish I was there (at the date). She's a real beautiful girl. I wouldn't mind going out with her if I have half a chance."

Jeff's family has been in on his career.

His mother at first was not keen on a music career for him, but seeing how determined he was, she does her best to support him.

His brother used to run the group's website—and started the group's fan club. There's dedication.

From all accounts the family is a down-to-earth and close-knit one, and probably part of the reason that Jeff has the courage to do the things he does is that he knew that if it all ended tomorrow, he could always go back home to people he loves.

What would he being doing now if he wasn't in 98°?

"I think we'd all be doing different things," he told *Galaxie* magazine. "I was in school, three of us were in school, but I can't speak for anybody else, but I'd still be in school." He laughed at that. "I like working with children, and I might have gotten a teaching degree or something like that."

However, with the kind of success that Jeff Timmons and the guys have gotten, it looks as though they'll be singing for a long, long time!

COMFORT JEFF

"It was the worst," Jeff Lachey told *BB* magazine. "I had a girl that I went out with for four years, then she decided she

liked another guy and broke up with me and I had to see her
with this guy every day when I went to school. That was the
worst feeling!''

As you can tell, the boys have paid their dues. They didn't
always have singles burning up the charts. They've had singles burning them!

And now, of course, with big hit records and plenty of
attention from the opposite sex as well as from music lovers
everywhere, you'd think that it's all peaches and cream, easy
street and Disneyland for Jeff Lachey.

The awful dumping Jeff speaks about above was in high
school and, though it was years ago, he still carries the scars.
You can't help but think that lots of the pain you hear in
songs like ''Invisible Man'' and ''Was It Something I didn't
Say'' and ''She's Out of My Life'' come from personal experience.

Let's find out a little more about Jeff.

Maybe, if we ever meet him, we can make him feel better.

JEFF CHAT

Here's a secret about Jeff that only certain people know.

Jeff likes to go into online chat rooms under a different
identity and talk to 98° fans.

That's right.

For those of you who don't know about the 98° chat
rooms, in which you can talk via your computer and share
notes with other 98° Fans, get to the chapter on websites later
in the book. (I'd put a link here, but books don't work that
way.)

For the merely curious, though, let's just say that chat
rooms on America Online and on the Internet itself allow you
to assume an identity (the name you call yourself) and engage
in typed conversation with other folks in the ''room.''

Well it appears that mischievous Jeff is not exactly too
busy with music, touring, doing PR visits, watching 99 cent
movies or girls in the flesh to not check out his cyberfans.

One of the first things that people who have met him talk about is his laugh.

Apparently, Jeff laughs and smiles a lot. You can see it in the pictures and tapes of him. You can imagine him, hunkering behind his I-Mac or his IBM Thinkpad notebook, plugged into the Internet, engaged in a conversation with his fans under his secret ID.

Knowing Jeff, he probably insists that 98° sucks, and the 'N Sync and Backstreet Boys rule! (Then giggles when outraged fans tell him he's full of malarkey.)

Jeff was the first of the Deegs to become computer literate. Rumor has it he had to show the others how to get online. But even though this smacks of innocent fun, you can't help but see how much Jeff appreciates his fans and takes what they say very seriously.

Once, when he revealed who he actually was, a fan engaged him in conversation for a while in a way that meant a lot to Jeff. Later, he actually called the fan up on the phone and thanked her for her support. They spoke for over an hour and Jeff proved to be such a sweetheart, the fan could not believe it. He was a gentleman, and listened to all her thoughts about the group, what they were good at and how maybe they could improve. He made the fan feel very special indeed.

Today, though, when you get into an online chat involving 98°, just be aware—One of the fans might be Jeff Lachey!

SAD AND LONELY GUY

One of the hardest things about being on the road all the time is that although you get to meet all kinds of people, it's hard to stay close to one special sweetheart.

That's why all the guys not only are single . . .

They apparently don't have steady girlfriends!

"We are all very, very single," Justin asserts.

Can you imagine?

This gorgeous hunk without a girlfriend?

Jeff must feel kind of down and lonely sometimes without a special someone that he can share his deepest self with.

If you got a chance to be around Jeff a bit, what do you think you could do to make him feel warm and loved?

How would you get his body temperature back up to 98°?

SOME TIME WITH JEFF

Can you imagine what it might be like if you got a chance to talk to Jeff in a 98° chat room?

Suppose he was feeling bad, and something you said cheered him up? You got to talking, and decided to talk for a bit in your own private chat room.

Jeff's a nice guy. He'd want to know all about you. He'd also probably want to make sure you liked 98° better than 'N Sync or Backstreet Boys.

"Well, I do kinda like 'Tearin' up My Heart,' " you might admit.

"Good," Jeff might say. "I like that in a person. Honesty."

Maybe he likes 'N Sync too!

All those guys party at music awards shows and the like, it's all cool. (Of course no one sings harmony like our guys—and no other blue-eyed-boy soul singers have got the R-and-B groovemasters at Motown behind them!)

So he calls you up!

"Hi," he may well say. "I was just feeling blue and you seem like such a nice person. I just want to talk a bit. What would you like to talk about?"

Sure, okay, yes, this is a fantasy . . .

But what if it happened?

What would you tell Jeff about yourself?

Well, of course, only you would know that, but Jeff sort of half expects fans to know about him these days.

(This hasn't always been so, but when they went over to play in Europe and Asia, the guys were stunned and flattered to find out that many of their fans know all about them!)

It was a status symbol for them. At first 98° wondered where the heck they'd gotten the info, but then they realized an amazing thing about today's world! Things are a lot closer, thanks to the Internet!)

So, do you know all about Jeff?

Do you know what he likes—what his favorite things are?

If not, let's get you all straight, okay?

Just in case Jeff should call!

DEEP JEFF FACTS

When he opens his heart up, singing his lead on "Because of You" you can't help but feel like Jeff is right there with you, telling you how he feels.

Feelings are terribly important, of course.

Facts, though, are vital. You can tell that Jeff's a soulful, feeling guy, but you need to know a little more about him than that he dances well and that he sings like an angel!

I guess you can pretty much guess what Jeff's favorite kind of music is. That's right. Rhythm and blues. Good ol' R and B. And it's not like he just started listening to it because he thought he could sing it and be a star. No way! He's an honest-to-goodness fan. You remember that the guys wanted to get to the backstage of the Boyz II Men show? It wasn't just to get noticed. Jeff wanted to meet that group. (He since has—and has gotten along well with them.)

No, you can't listen to Jeff sing and not realize that he loves the kind of music he and the guys are singing.

Other bands he loves include Take 6 and Jodeci—but dollars to doughnut holes, if you showed him a list of all the soul and R and B groups, he'd bob his head and grin and say "Yes, yes, yes!"

So if you know the difference between Sly and Family Stone, and Smokey Robinson and the Miracles, that sure would impress Jeff. And boy, if you happened to know that it was Smokey and not the Temptations who wrote the amazing "My Girl."

But you should also know that Jeff is a definite carnivore. He really enjoys a good steak, apparently, and his next favorite dinner is seafood. (So, he probably eats a lot of surf and turf—at least if he's at that sort of restaurant.)

Jeff would love to go to New Zealand and Australia . . . not necessarily to sing . . . just to see those places!

Here's another important fact: Jeff loves football. In fact, at one time Jeff dreamed of playing professional football. Now, he still probably kicks some pigskin around with the guys sometimes—or with friends and neighbors in pick-up games—but he gets closer to professional football than most people these days, because he and the guys sometimes sing their *a cappella* version of "The Star Spangled Banner" at pro football games.

Even though it's Drew that gripes about being short, Jeff's not that much taller, as five foot eight.

His hair is brown (untouched as yet by dye, although when the guys go through their glam period, who knows).

His eyes are quite blue.

How blue are his eyes?

So blue, that he was voted as having the prettiest eyes in his senior class.

He used to weigh less, but lately he's beefed himself up incredibly. Nick is no longer the only beefcake boy in this band! In fact, if you look at the pictures here and elsewhere, or get treated to a show in which the guys whip off their shirts you get an eyeful.

Jeff is buff!

At interviews where there are young ladies present, many seem to be ogling his build. On an Internet chat, one young lady enthused that she thought he looked fine.

Indeed, Jeff has been keeping up a regular health regimen lately. Lifting weights and generally working out whenever possible must be difficult with his schedule, but its benefits are obvious.

A recent issue of *Popstar* magazine seemed happy to unveil a half-dressed Jeff.

Obviously, he's proud of his physique.

Apparently, at the time when he was thinking about doing that professional football thing, he was at about 200 pounds (and not flab). Really big. But, after they signed with Motown, he lost a lot of weight.

What? From learning dance steps?

In any case, since then he's built himself back up, but to no where near that 200 pounds. Instead, he's been working out and he finds that now he's in a lot better shape.

Now he pushes those weights at least twice a week. (With those biceps and pecs, I'd say more than that!) His prescriptions for big muscles: heavy weights and low reps (repetions). He also credits stretching with keeping him toned.

When he's watching football on TV (or in the stands, preferably) he mostly likes to watch the Dallas Cowboys.

He digs Robert De Niro in films and goes for Selma Hayek as an actress.

His favorite movie is *The Shawshank Redemption*.

No product placement here, but Jeff really digs Phat Farm clothes. (What—no other kinds like the others—is Phat Farm to Jeff Lachey like J. Crew is to *Dawson's Creek*? Not likely. Anyway, do they have a catalog? Are they way, way into the color black?)

Needless to say, if you've been looking much at the pictures of the guys hither and yon (and here!) 98° and Jeff Lachey are heavily, heavily into the monochrome look. Of course that's the city look—urban guys like black. Why?

Simple.

It looks good. Leather feels and looks great and it's best if it's black. Black will always be fashionable. Plus, its easy to match socks. . . .

But can you imagine if, one show, Jeff came out wearing a blue shirt and orange pants? Ughh!

Well, honestly, this is not Elton John here!

In fact, orange and blue are Jeff's favorite colors. But just because he enjoys a little touch of tangerine and aqua in his life from time to time, doesn't necessarily mean that he's going to start becoming the Mr. Rainbow of 98°.

Promise!

TATOOS AND A BIG SECRET

You can tell from his interviews (and from his shows) that Jeff is pretty much a big ham.

He loves life.

He loves to laugh.

That laugh is something that all 98° fans remember if they're lucky enough to get close to him.

The hamminess, oops, I mean dramatic ability, goes way back in life. He's been into drama for a while. Remember that "Rising Star" award back at school?

Well, it's not all he shows off at shows, or at signings, if the guests are lucky.

He's got at least two tattoos—anyway, two tattoos that you can see if he takes off his shirt.

The first is on his right arm. It just says 98°, but it's very important to him.

"My 98° tattoo is because even if it all ended today, the band means a lot to my life," he told *Pop Star* magazine.

But that wasn't Jeff's first tattoo.

No, the first one is right above his heart.

On his left pectoral he's got some Japanese characters that translate to "heaven" and "good luck." I don't think that Jeff is particularly superstitious but, as tattoos are in these days, it's better than "Mom" or a great big heart with a knife stuck through it!

Or can you imagine Jeff with a belly-button ring?

Naw. Let's stick with the tattoos and enjoy them.

Jeff is not only a candid person about his skin decorations. He's happy to let you know in no uncertain terms exactly what his failings are.

For instance, he's a bit of a klutz.

For example, at a show that 98° gave in Phoenix, Jeff spotted a girl he wanted to sing to in particular. The song going was "Invisible Man" and, clearly, Jeff wanted to make sure that he was quite visible to this female. So he thought—

Hey! What about some audience participation! He was heading out into the audience, those blue, blue eyes trained on one lucky girl.

Can you conjure up the scene!

The drama is up high and thousands of people are watching his every move as he sings the sad song about how he wishes that someone loved him. Oh, the sighs of his admirers! The sounds of gasps as many, many female hearts cried out: "I see you! I see you Jeff!"

So here's Jeff, star of the moment, and he's headed down the stairs. And he's crooning out his feelings and the girl eats it all up, and the audience—well, it's just in the palm of his hand. Cool and confident, he turns back and walks back up the stairs, headed for the stage and the spotlight so that everyone will get the full impact of his Jeff-ness.

And . . . ooops!

He put his foot down wrong. He slipped. And the royal tenor tattooed one fell flat on his face in front of thousands, sprawling out and probably even losing the thread of the song!

That must have been something to see!

If Jeff is klutzy, then maybe you might see him make a boo-boo or two if you catch the 98° stage act. But, with all the practice they've been getting and the new choreography, chances are that the show will be pretty polished so don't get your hopes up.

Just know that Jeff is as human as anybody and probably has a pratfall or two behind the scenes.

He's also the messy one of the group.

While the others—especially Drew—are pretty neat and tidy, Jeff is . . .

Well, what's the polite word for it?

Scattered?

The guys rag on him all the time about it in interviews, but Jeff just laughs his big laugh and says exactly what is the truth to him, like the quote he gave to the *YTV* Interview:

"I'm not messy . . . I'm just disorganized!"

Yeah, yeah, Jeff.

You're a guy and guys are just like that sometimes, right?

In fact, he's so normal; he's revealed that in a rather astonishing story.

For such a handsome and cool guy, he's not only had the difficult love life I mentioned before—His first date was an absolute disaster!

Hard to think that's the case, but it's true. Jeff has said that the first time he ever went out with a girl, nothing went right. Evidently, he was a teenager, and the date was made by his mother.

Apparently Mom and her best friend were playing matchmaker, because they got the best friend's daughter and Jeff together.

Alas, "the girl didn't dig him at all."

It's hard to imagine why, but, then again, even though Jeff is polished and self-confident now, it doesn't mean he's always been that way.

Not only that, but once, in those early days, Jeff serenaded a girl with "Unchained Melody," and she advised him never to sing again.

Thank goodness he didn't take her advice, huh?

(Although from the sounds of it, those who are treated to Jeff getting ready for a show might wish so—apparently he warms up for a concert by singing "Yawo Yawo Yawo" out of tune, loudly.)

Anyway, if a girl could deal with a klutzy guy who does that, what would she look for in a date with Jeff?

DATING JEFF

One day Jeff was just walking along, being himself. Maybe he was humming or he was thinking about an arrangement of a new song the group was doing . . . but anyway, his mind was pretty much on other matters, so he didn't notice that someone had noticed him.

It was a girl.

The girl apparently knew exactly who this guy in Phat

Farm clothes was, and she had an immediate and very emotional reaction.

Without warning, the girl ran up to him, threw her arms around his neck and kissed him.

Well, true, she got to touch Jeff. Problem was, that although Jeff was polite about the whole thing and probably even agreed to sign an autograph, that was about it.

Actually, as he revealed later, he was upset. No way was this a great way to meet a girl. Much too forward.

Jeff is much more a traditional kind of guy. Of course, he's red-blooded male and he likes to kiss girls just as much as any guy (maybe even more!) But he likes to know who the girl is first.

He's said that he's a pretty standard dater. A first date might go like this:

He'd bring some flowers for the girl. (Blue and orange flowers? Unlikely. With Jeff being way traditional and all, roses would probably be his choice. And more than one! Jeff's making more money these days!)

Dinner. (Steak or seafood for him, of course, but you know, he's probably the kind of guy who would let the girl say where she'd like to eat.)

A movie. (Although he likes De Niro and Hayek a lot, the way Jeff laughs, he would probably want to go to a comedy. I'm getting definite vibes that Jeff could well be the kind of guy who would go for *Something about Mary* or *Dumb and Dumber* . . . Big yucks movies, you know.

And a kiss on a the first date.

Yes, true, it looks as though he's got a very kissable mug, so maybe that would be okay. But don't be surprised if Jeff doesn't want to, because, you know . . .

He's been burned before.

In fact, when he was interviewed for Canadian TV and was asked exactly what he was singing about, Jeff pretty much laid it on the line:

"Love. Relationships."

What does he look for in girls that he might do that dinner and movie thing with?

"I don't have a specific type (of girl he likes)," he told an AOL chat room. "I'm single. I just like girls that are fun to be around and have a sense of humor."

And if you were wondering if there's any room for romance in Jeff's life, look what he told Exan later on in that Canadian interview:

"I'm Jeff. I'm single. I'm looking for a girlfriend, so if there are any girls out there—"

Okay. We'd like to think that Jeff would be more discerning than to go for just any girl . . .

But you know what . . .

Don't you just get the smidgen of a feeling that Jeff is one guy who likes to flirt?

Well, nothing wrong with that.

But wait. There are a couple of things that he likes that seem very important:

"I usually look for a girl with beautiful eyes and a great sense of humor," he clarified to Exan.

Well, we knew the humor bit, but the eyes—that helps.

He's also not necessarily just a dinner and movies guy, it would seem.

"I just want the opportunity to get a chance to talk to the girl. Not necessarily go any place in particular the first couple of dates. Just get to know the person and wherever it leads from there, start going that way."

Well, lets fade out on that a bit.

Let's see what other people think about what you'd find out about Jeff, if you got to know him.

Really know him.

THE REAL JEFF

The guys are singing.

Let's say they're singing "Under the Boardwalk," a great four-part harmony oldie that lots of the doo-wop groups of the fifties and sixties used to sing.

If one of the guys is just a little bit off key . . . Jeff's the one to catch it first.

Jeff can tell what's in tune and what's out of tune.

He's kind of like that in life.

"Jeff is . . ." Justin Jeffre told *Popstar*, "I'd say he's kinda spiritual, one of the more chipper guys in the band."

Here's what he wrote in the liner notes of the *98° and Rising* CD:

"Thank you God and St. Jude for your continuous blessings. My family, Jim, Trish, Michael and Kristina Timmons, Bob and Irene Marchione, Olga Timmons (My Angel Above), Trish (My Angel on Earth), you are all my inspiration—I love you. Darby and Jolene, the Fechters, the McCarthy's, the Skelly's, Waggoner, Thad King, Ron Humphrey, Kenny Weber, Paris and Johnny (The Goodfellas!) Less—Thanks man, 98°—Love and God Bless always. To our fans—you're the world's best."

Jeff Timmons, always laughing if he's not singing, has one thing about him that will always be true.

Jeff's a big sweetie, with a big, big heart.

Oh, and he loves that Skyline Chili, too!

Second Degree:
Nick Lachey

"I just lost my girlfriend recently," a sad Nick Lachey, lead singer for 98° reported to *Teen Celebrity* magazine. "And what's frustrating is that it was almost an inevitable thing. It wasn't that we weren't meant for each other—we were together for six years—it's that both of us realized we needed to make certain sacrifices for our careers."

This is the kind of depth and honesty that the handsome, hunky Nick gives to his fans. It's also what he gives to his music. Who can doubt that when he sings "Because of You" with that throbbing, high and yet supremely masculine voice, that he means every single word of it!

Where did this kind of character and talent come from?

Let's look closer at the life behind the personality.

BLUEGRASS SOUL

Nicholas Scott Lachey was born November 9, 1973 in Harlan, Kentucky, home of bluegrass music.

He was the first of his parents' brood, which later came to include brother Drew, half-brother Issac, adopted brother Zac and adopted sisters Josie and Katlin.

Like Justin and Drew, Nick attended the Creative School for the Performing Arts—a place that graduated a number of stars.

(In fact, check out that website "Before They Were Famous" in the 98° website section for some great pictures of Nick in high school!)

While in school, Nick learned to play the saxophone—so don't be surprised if, sometime, at a 98° concert, Nick pulls out a sax and starts blowing some back-up honks!

While in school Nick was an extra in the movie *Odd Men Out*, a film by John Sayles about the infamous Cincinnati Black Sox in 1919. You have to look closely for him, because he's hard to spot—but he's there! Some sources claim that brother Drew is in the movie as well, but experts say that's not the case.

Also, if Nick looks a bit like a handsome running back, it's for good reason. He played football in high school and college. He was such a dedicated athlete, in fact, that his choice of majors in college seemed a natural.

At Miami University of Ohio, Nick studied sports medicine. Still, he'd been singing since a very young age, and sang in high school musicals. He'd sung with lots of people and was known for his nice, mellow voice.

So when he got the call from Jeff that fateful day, he was ready, even though the call was unexpected.

When he did a little bit of singing, Jeff was sold.

"How'd you like to come and be in a group with me?" Jeff said.

Jeff's energy and enthusiasm must have been very persuasive indeed. Either that, or Nick had been dreaming of just such an opportunity. In any case, Nick was soon out in Los Angeles.

Of course, it wasn't like he was wealthy or anything. Jeff had warned him that he'd have to work at odd hours to keep body and spirit together while they did their singing around town and worked toward a break. So Nick delivered Chinese food.

Back in Ohio he also had worked at an amusement arcade. "Fun for about two minutes," Nick confides. But, basically, all these odd jobs were always to keep himself together while he sang.

Singing is his first love.

He and Justin have sung in a barbershop quartet, and a doo-wop group, The Avenues, for a while. Ever since high school, in fact.

And suppose 98° had never happened? What would Nick be doing now?

"Probably be graduated now. Singing in a local band with Justin, or a sports trainer," he told an Asian net chat.

Nick's the dreamer of the group, the sensitive and touching singer whose heart goes out with his tender voice.

"Nick is so talented. He's probably the best singer in the group," Jeff Timmons has said.

The yearning, sweet and intimate sound of Nick Lachey's voice will doubtless be filling the stereo speakers of young and old for many, many years to come.

A Date with Nick

Imagine you're a young woman working late at the office. You're starving, but the manager wants you to finish this report so he can take it with him tonight when he catches the red-eye to Boston for an important sales conference.

You're starving, though, but you don't have time to go out. You feel like having some Chicken Moo Goo Gai Pan, so you pull out the menu from the local Chinese spot that delivers and you place the call.

Minutes later, standing there is a hunky guy, holding a steaming bag of Chinese goodies, blue eyes looking at you appreciatively. He's a little sweaty from hurrying over and he smells like sweet oolong tea.

And he's soooo cute!

The radio's turned to an oldies station and he hums along to Frankie Valli and the Four Seasons as you dig out the money to pay him, making sure he gets a nice tip. You're too nervous to say, Oh my god, you're so gorgeous! So you compliment him on his nice voice.

"Oh, yeah! I'm in Los Angeles with a new R-and-B group," he might say. "We're looking for our first break!"

Sing your favorite song for me, you say.

And Nick Lachey, sings "In the Still of the Night."

Gosh, his voice goes high!

Fantasy? Nope. This really happened. And Nick liked the girl too, he told a magazine. She was very pretty.

He had her number, but "I didn't have the nerve to call her. Singing is easy. But otherwise I can be shy."

Nick?

Shy?

Sure. You have to remember, that even though he croons sexily and confidently on the 98° recordings, that's singing, and he's had a lots of coaching, practice—and maybe he's on the tenth take of the song, at that!

Even though it sounds as though he knows just what to do to get his arms around a girl, and just what to do with his lips when he gets close—

In reality, that big heart would probably be pounding hard and he'd be perspiring and stuttering because he was nervous.

So you'd just have to hold him and tell him that it was all right, that it was all right to be nervous and shy . . .

And then you'd hold him closer and . . .

Fantasy alert!

Alarm!

Do not heat up past 98°!

Nick, Relaxed

Actually, Nick looks more like a jock than than a singing star! In fact, Nick is a huge sports buff. Since he played football in high school he probably likes to goof around with balls from time to time in between gigs, signing autographs and chatting with fans, and doing the soulful barbership thing with the guys in the group.

Nick is a loyal sports fan, and his favorite teams are the Cincinnati Bengals (football) and the Cincinnati Reds (baseball).

Nick also digs basketball, which is why the following helps him out in his sports love:

At five foot eleven inches, he's the biggest of the group. (Any time you see the guys in a picture together, he's always sticking out like the Empire State Building on the Manhattan skyline.)

Sure, he'd have a hard time going one-on-one with Charles Barkley, but with little brother Drew, well, that wouldn't be quite so hard.

Although he can't always play sports, he keeps himself in the great shape he's in by working out with free weights and other kinds of exercise equipment. (It was Nick who was way buff first, but it would seem as though Jeff was inspired, because Jeff Timmons has certainly been headed into the same kind of muscular territory!)

What kind of food does Nick pack into building up those slabs of abs and reps of biceps?

Well, pretty much what the other guys eat—lots of Skyline Chili!

But his favorite food also includes steak, pizza and barbeque, all members of the necessary 98° food groups. (You wonder if Nick tucks in three steaks a day like Jeff says he often does, but then, even though Nick's had those righteous muscles for a while, he's not necessarily building up.)

So send in the pizza, guys!

Gotta pack in the carbs!

(Nick loves to joke. When someone asked him on an AOL chat how he got his muscles, he answered:

"Goat's milk. How else?"

Although he probably downs those special work-out energy drinks when he's pushing the weights or playing basketball or football, his favorite drink is actually Yoo Hoo.

Must be a Cincinnati thing.

He too is waaay into Phat Farm clothing when he's not in his sweats or his workout Ts and shorts. (And he's in them a lot—working out and playing sports are things he really, really enjoys doing.)

He also enjoys relaxing with some TV or some movies, and his favorite stars are Bruce Willis and Michele Pfieffer.

What's the first movie he's getting in DVD format?

Probably *Die Hard*.

His favorite color?

Red!

What physical possession does Nick value the most? Why, his stereo, of course.

Nick's life revolves around music, and not just professionally.

His favorite music that he plays on that stereo (and it must be a pretty sharp one now, what with all his success!) are the CDs of Boyz II Men, Brian McKnight, Jodeci—and, of course, lots and lots of R and B.

You can just tell that Nick knows the music by listening to him sing.

NICK'S TALENT

It's Nick that sings most leads on the songs, although he trades off sometimes with Jeff, who's no slouch in that department.

Still, Nick can sing high and soulful without going falsetto. (Think the Bee Gees!)

More than that, he knows exactly what to do with his voice.

Listen to one of the songs of one his idols, Brian McKnight—"The Way Love Goes" from the CD *Brian McKnight*. McKnight's voice wavers and flys and soars with the melody. (We'll talk about McKnight and his influence on the group later.) This is a quality that urban soul singers must have, and Nick's tenor has got the stuff it takes to sing this kind of music.

How did he get his voice—and his brain—to be able to do this?

Well, for one thing, being a professional singer has always

been the top dream in Nick's aspirations. As you may recall, he was in a lot of drama throughout school—and often appeared in musicals, so he had lots of practice actually getting up in front of people and belting out songs.

However, the biggest thing to happen to Nick vocally was in high school.

That was when he first heard Take 6.

Take 6 is an *a cappella* group. That, of course, means they sing without instruments. (Check out the section about them further on in the book.)

Nick loved to sing so much and was such a fan that he got himself backstage at a Take 6 concert (you have to wonder now if it was Nick's idea to try and get backstage at that Boyz II Men show).

It had been a terrific show, and Nick couldn't help but tell the guys in Take 6 how much he wanted to be a pro singer, how much he wanted to do what they did.

Apparently Nick's dream was always being in a group, not being a solo singer.

Take 6 were very encouraging.

"They told me," Nick says, "The only way to do good harmony is to keep trying and practicing. Just keep going."

Keep going he has, and now look at where he is!

(Just listen to Take 6 backing up "My Friend" for Ray Charles on their *Join the Band* CD, and you'll see what we mean about absolutely great harmony singing!)

Singing with a great group called 98°.

But really . . . listen to Nick's voice. It's not only talented—it's velvet and soft and strong and vulnerable and so, so expressive.

Listening to Nick Lachey sing the songs of 98°—whether it's "Invisible Man" or "Something I Didn't Say" from their first CD or "Because of You" or "The Hardest Thing" from their second, you just have to think—

He're one sensitive guy.

In fact, Nick Lachey is just that.

NICK'S SOUL

The songs get to Nick.

There are lots of emotions in 98° songs, and when Nick Lachey sings—when he talks about feeling as though the girl he loves doesn't even see him—or he wishes that he'd told a departed sweetheart that he loved her—or regrets losing the best thing in his life, his girlfriend—he actually feels the sentiments expressed in the song.

An example.

One of the best songs from the guys first CD is "Heaven's Missing an Angel."

" 'Heaven's Missing an Angel' is such a beautiful song," Nick says. "Everytime I hear it, I have to smile. It just brings something deep out of me."

Nick is a pretty deep guy and he's got a lot of feelings.

One of the deepest relationships he's got is with his little brother Drew, who sings baritone.

Their beloved grandmother was dreadfully worried about young Drew when he joined 98°, and she expressed that worry to Nick. Nick swore to her that he'd take care of Drew. Watch over the guy. Now that his grandmother has passed on, he feels particularly concerned about Drew.

Of course, in every brotherly relationship, there's always that good ol' sibling rivalry. He's said some funny things about Drew, but they have dealt with the brother thing well.

"We got over that (sibling rivalry) before the group got together. Now we're more best friends than anything else. I mean, we get on each other's nerves sometimes, but no more than Jeff and I get on each other's nerves. We're all like a big family anyway."

But basically he's solidly behind his little bro:

"He's a great singer and great performer, so just the chance to work with him on that level is good," he told *Pop Star* magazine.

"I also like that we get to spend time together. Most broth-

"The boys in the band, seen here in the back of a limousine, always travel in style."

"With one seductive stare, the men of 98° can launch their female fans into a frenzy."

"Looking like GQ cover models, Drew, Nick, Jeff and Justin pose for the camera."

"**Drew and Jeff flash their winning smiles at an autograph signing.**"

© Desiree DiCristoforo, Shooting Star

© Desiree DiCristoforo, Shooting Star

"Nick and Justin take a break from their busy schedules to sign a few autographs and win over new fans."

"At Nickelodeon's
5th Annual
Help-A-Thon, 98°
sing their hearts out
for a good cause."

"Whether dressed to impress or dressed down, one thing's for sure.

The boys of 98° always look HOT."

"98° get their first taste of stardom at the Mulan premiere."

ers at this age might be living in different cities and see each other only on the holidays. It's great because we're there for each other. It's an 'I got your back' kind of thing.''

The guys have had some problems sometimes, once with a girl when they were both in their teens.

Seems that they both had crushes on the same girl.

Drew was dating the girl first, but then the girl decided that she liked Nick better, and dumped Drew.

Although he felt bad about dating a girl that his brother had such feelings for, he couldn't help himself. Nick had big, big feelings for the girl and was under her spell.

Unfortunately, not long afterwards, the fickle girl decided that she liked someone better than Nick and—WHAM!

Nick found himself suddenly in the high-school dump, right beside his little brother.

Well, they'd probably been through worse before—after all, after Nick's playing Ebenezer Scrooge to Drew's Tiny Tim in *A Christmas Carol*, you have to know that they'd get through thick and thin.

You have to wonder what happens if they both like the same girl now.

Fortunately (or unfortunately), it's very hard to keep up relationships while you're flying around all over the world, so they don't have girlfriends around to dump or be dumped by. However what happens if they meet a snazzy lady they both like? Do they flip a coin?

Well, that's between them, actually. (Some things are private, you know!)

Nonetheless, Nick's sensitivity must keep him pretty much close to the other guys, so that kind of disruption probably would never happen again.

Besides, now that these guys are much more mature, much more handsome—and much more popular!—and there are any number of girls around, right?

Well, actually, knowing Nick, he's not that much into strings of girlfriends. You get the definite sense that he's likely to have one special person to be close to. One special girl to relax with, to share his deepest feelings with, to have candlelit dinners with and listen to soft R and B with in some romantic, rose-scented setting.

But, the question remains: Just what sort of girl would Nick think was Ms. Right?

Let's see, shall we?

NICK AT NIGHT

He's all alone now.

It's been rough, being out touring, and he's back home now and very, very tired. So tired, he's slept way, way late into the morning. Now, he's sprawled in his sheets, feeling kinda drowsy, wondering if there's a Yoo Hoo in the refrigerator.

Nick's sprawled out, wearing only his boxer shorts and his tattoos. He's got plenty of girls' phone numbers, written on napkins and underwear thrown to him on the stage, and his book is filled with girls' phone numbers.

But Nick feels bad.

Nick feels lonely.

All of the girls seem like terrific people and he really appreciates the fact that they adore 98°, they love his music and they think he's fantastic.

None of them are that special someone—

But what are the criteria, Nick?

"I like a girl for her personality," Nick told an AOL chatter. "I'm pretty open to dating any kind of girl."

Yes, but what kind of personality, Nick?

"I'm looking for a girl who's beautiful in every sense of the word—her personality, has a great sense of humour, fun to be around."

Dear me. Nick's got to be meeting those kinds of girls every day! It's not like there aren't lots of girls.

Probably the big problem is that Nick doesn't stay in one place for very long. When you're in a pop group you're constantly on the move. Even when you live in one place! Nick and the guys live in New York now, but New York is one busy place. Nick is probably constantly on the move even in the Big Apple.

So, it's hard to sit down and concentrate on someone to see, even if they had that right combination of humor and spark and beauty—that right person to make the connection that Nick's looking for.

But, suppose Nick does meet a girl, and not only does the girl like him—he likes the girl!

How would he go about dating her?

Well, yeah, ask her out, sure.

But what would Nick like to do on those dates?

"I like," Nick said on that AOL chat "especially on the first couple of dates when you're just getting to know somebody, to go out to a nice long dinner so you have an opportunity to talk and you get to know each other really well. I don't really like to go to movies or anything, because there's no interaction really. So, a nice long dinner."

It doesn't sound like we have an aloof guy who doesn't like to get close to girls, does it.

But what would you find out about what Nick is really like—deep down?

True Nick

"I've been friends with Nick for a long time," Justin Jeffre told *Popstar* magazine, "so I can say that he's either the comedy or the guy who's stressing out the most, kind of like the guy who will be upset for a week if his football team loses!"

Drew Lachey considers Nick to be the group spokesman. Drew jokingly refers to Nick as a "natural loudmouth." According to the 98° baritone, even when you don't agree with what Nick is saying, the way he phrases things makes you think about the subject.

Jeff Timmons echoes these thoughts.

"Nick is a great talent," he told *Pop star*, "but he's got

great leadership qualities and he's passionate about what he does.''

What are Nick's ambitions?

"To be successful at whatever I attempt to do," he says.

One of those dreams that Nick has is to start some kind of sports franchise with the 98° folk. Wow! With all their success now, it looks as though that dream is becoming not only a possibility but a probability!

But it's not just business that concerns Nick. He thinks a lot about the band and what it can do.

"Twenty years from now, I'd like to think that 98° will leave a lasting impression."

Well, their music and personalities are certainly making a dent. But they're already helping out lots with contributions of time, energy—and money—to various charities important to them.

Why wait? Let's get back to Nick.

An insight into the real Nick is available right in the liner notes of *98° and Rising*:

"Firstly and most importantly I'd like to thank the Lord for continuing to guide my life. I would like to thank my family—Mom, Dad, Iris, Jeff, Isaac, Josei, Zach, Caitlin and all the Lacyesy's, Fompa's, Staley's and Leimbachs. I love all of you and appreciate your constant support. Devon, Andre and Bonecutter—it's been a BIG year for all of us! To Rochyel—you've always been there through thick and thin. Thanks! You know I'll ways love you. A big shout out to Paris and Jonny at Top 40 Entertainment. Much love to Oler, Lippman, Sami, Murai, Dawn, Lee Ann, Lisa C., Miami U. SAE. The Avenues and fans, Forte and SCPA. Finally—Jeff, Justin, Drew. We always knew it was gonna be a wild ride! I love you guys. 98° forever! To anyone I've overlooked, you know I'm an idiot. Thanks."

A pretty humble guy, eh?

Has success gone to that handsome head?

Nope.

The only problem is, he told *Teen Celebrity*:

"People don't realize you're still the same person. They

think you deserve special privileges, kind of place you on a pedestal.''

Normal Nick told an Asian magazine that his ultimate goal is to have a wife and family and do all the things for that family that they could possibly want.

When he appeared on the show *Loveline*, Nick listened carefully to all the people who called in and talked about their problems.

He's very handsome, yes, and he sings great. He had carefully though-out advice for them—and what was obviously very real and deep concern for his fellow human beings.

He's one terrific fellow.

So, when Nick sings about how sunny things are now, ''Because of You,'' and points out of that video . . . He's pointing right at you!

Third Degree:
Justin Jeffre

On their appearance on ABC's *The View*, Justin, 98°
bass singer was the funniest member of the group.

This was in early December '98 and you'd think that guys
would be tired, since they'd just gotten back from the Far
East and were in the middle of a whirlwind tour to promote
98° and Rising, but they all looked excited and enthusiastic
and bustling with energy. The guys sang their single, "Because of You," with Four-Tops-meet-hip-hop dance steps.
Now, these guys are only learning to dance, so you have to
admit they look pretty darned slick, considering—but, still,
the camera kept on catching Justin having difficulty slipping
his mike back into its stand so he could be ready to clap or
turn around or whatever. And when the hostess walked up
with the CD and suggested that it might make a good stocking
stuffer, Justin clearly felt that the audience couldn't see the
cover right, so he grabbed it from her and gave the camera a
better shot!

Bass and grace!

What a combo!

When did Justin first realize that he had a subwoofer in
his diaphragm that could do that kind of stuff?

"I was in choir at school singing soprano and alto," he
told *Pop Star* magazine. "When I came back one summer,
they put me into the bass section!"

Justin Paul Jeffre was born on February 25, 1973 in Mount

Clemens, Michigan, and grew up in the Finneytown area of Cincinnati.

He had a fairly normal boyhood and has been singing as long as he can remember.

What does he think of when he thinks of Cincinnati?

"Cincinnati has some of the best ice cream in the world," he told an Asian magazine.

One of his memories of childhood was a little unusual: "The first time driving a car, when I was only 9 years old."

So you have to hope that it was on some private property and not on the highway!

Justin's always been a high-spirited fellow.

You can see what he looked like in high school by going to website. That would be: http://tinpan.fortunecity.com/blondie/195/justin.html.

If you can't make it, I'll clue you in.

The first picture that's available is from 1987, when Justin was in eighth grade. He looks like a confident young fellow, and one of the remarkable things is that the picture reveals that Justin has naturally curly hair! In his 98° photos, his hair is always pretty closely cropped. But, by looking at these pictures, we can see what it's really like.

In fact, the next picture is Justin, a little older, in music theatre. He's singing away, and his hair is flopping in front of his face, long and quite dashing.

The next is Justin's senior photo, hair a little shorter and looking just as confident and handsome. His main interest is stated as: vocal music.

It's Nick Lachey and Justin who've worked together longest. Well, maybe work isn't the right word because what they do, they love. Okay, they've sung together the longest. They met in Cincinnati's School for Creative Performing Arts. They were in Paramount's King Island Barber Shop together, and the R-and-B doo-wop group The Avenues.

You can imagine how Nick thought of Justin when Jeff Timmons needed a good bass guy for the group.

"I've got a really deep voice," he explained to *Big UK* magazine and had it even in his school days. "I talked to this guy on the phone when I was about 15 and he thought I was about 60.''

His life before 98°?

"I'm not sure I really had one," he told *Big UK*.

He was attending college when he got that momentous call from Nick.

Also, he has a family, including an older brother Dan, stepsister Ann, stepbrother Jeff and half-sister Alexandra.

What is known for sure is that his dream car is an Acura NSX.

And they way things are going for 98°, he'll be getting one for sure eventually—if he hasn't already got one!

Music is also the center of Justin's life.

But there are also other things that motivate him.

When asked by an Asian interviewer about what was on the slate for an upcoming tour of journey, Justin piped up right away.

"We're hoping to meet some German babes!" he said.

"Shut up, Justin!" cried Nick and Drew.

Let's look a little closer at what this guy with the big voice is like, in person.

JUST JUSTIN

Brrrppppppp!

Say what?

BRRRRRRRRRRRPPPPPPPPPPPP!

What's that sound?

An airplane? A guy pretending to be an airplane? A guy about to play a trumpet?

Nope!

It's just Justin Jeffre, warming up to sing!

You see, to get ready for practice, Justin vibrates his lips. That must create some din in the dressing room, while some makeup person is putting the final touches on that mellow face and a hairdresser is snipping off this and that to make his dyed-blond hair and goatee are as sharp as can be.

BRRRRPPPPPPPPP!

You wonder if that's what he does before he calls a girl.

Hello? Is this Kimberley? BRRRRRRRRP! This is Justin! BRRRRRRRRRRRP! Would you like to come with me to see a Jennifer Love Hewitt movie? BRRRRRRRRRRP!

You think I'm kidding?

Actually, I am, but this would not be the strangest thing that a singer or musician ever did to get ready for a show.

In case you forgot, Justin's the bass guy, whose low notes give that extra oomph to a vocal group like 98°. Yes, we know he can sing, yes, we know he can dance, yes we know some details about his life—

But what about his personality, what about his likes and dislikes, his fears and dreams?

Let's leave Justin's soul music for a moment . . . and get a little into Justin's soul.

Hangin' with Justin

It's Justin's deep, bluesy voice you hear at the beginning of the very first 98° CD, *98°*.

He introduces the members of the band, and he asks if you're ready for 98°—baby.

Can you imagine that voice talking to you on the phone?

Better yet, can you imagine you and Justin settling down on a couch with some popcorn and some pizza, some sodas, probably to watch a movie and then just chill and listen to some jazz. (That's Justin's absolutely favorite kind of music, although he, of course, loves R and B. I'm afraid that there's no way I'm going to be able to include a section on jazz here, but if you use the names Thelonious Monk, Miles Davis and Charlie Parker with awe once in a while, he'd like that. Oh— and since jump swing is in now, remember Louis Jordan. It will take you far!)

Then, maybe Justin will light some logs in the fireplace. He'll turn the lights down low. Then he'll sit on the couch next to you . . . edge closer . . . put his arm along the back of the couch near you. . . . You can smell CK perfume, rich and musky . . .

"Baby . . ." he'll say. "Baby . . ." in that rich dusky voice of his that make your insides just melt. You're feeling a little dizzy and you're glad you're sitting, because your knees are getting weak.

"Baby, would you like to hear the new 98° demo?"

You bet you would!

So he gets up to get the demo and some more popcorn.

Justin's a romantic, sure, but he wouldn't want to take advantage of someone on the first date!

THIS AND THAT

Yes, Justin loves jazz.

But, at heart, like the Blues Brothers, he's a soul man.

"I love the funky music of James Brown," he told the 98° home page. "He is my idol. When we opened for him it was a dream come true."

That was back in the early days, before 98° were even signed.

Justin's also a huge fan of Stevie Wonder, Marvin Gaye, and Sade. You can't help but think that he's got some Barry White in his collection as well.

His eyes are blue and the actual color of his hair under that blond dye job now is brown. (Me, I like the blond, don't you?)

If he's not working or sleeping and the TV is on, chances are that if Justin has his say, the set is turned to *60 Minutes* or *20/20* or some other news or educational program. That's the Justin who was the history major in college, remember? That's the Justin who's concerned about the state of the world, and current events. He feels that a knowledge of history is essential to know what's going on today.

Justin's just a very concerned cat.

"Justin drags us all out and make us see the cities we're in," points out Drew in *Popstar.*

Clearly, Justin is really enjoying the travel the group is doing.

One place that 98° hasn't been yet that Justin would like to visit is Africa. He is particularly interested in Central Africa, where he'd like to go on a safari.

He's also loves to travel to Sante Fe, New Mexico and always finds it a gas to return to the exciting Los Angeles where the boys got discovered. (They live in New York City, now, remember . . . but I'm sure they get to go back to Los Angeles lots.)

When he's not watching relevant shows on TV, he'll probably watch sports—his favorite team is the Cincinnati Bengals (loyal lad!).

But it sounds as though he'd rather play than watch!

Sports he enjoys playing?

Try soccer and tennis.

Running around kicking a big ball with his feet or running around hitting a small ball with a racket (and now dancing with 98°) must be what keeps Justin down to 150 pounds on his five foot ten inch frame, because his favorite foods seem to be pizza and doughnuts—washed down with iced tea, presumably mixed with lots of sugar.

Nicknames?

The guys call him "Droopy" or "Big J" when they're messing around.

("Hey Droopy!" You can almost hear Nick saying. "You can't sing low with a doughnut in your mouth while you're kicking a soccer ball around!")

"Big J! How did the date go last night? Get past first base?" Drew might shout. "You did? Oh you went to a baseball game!"

Most likely he went on that date wearing Ralph Lauren clothes—or maybe DKNY or Phat Farm duds.

And chances are very good that he'd be wearing blue because that's Justin's favorite color.

(Of course, in most of the pictures we see he's in black—but that's just the current fashion for hip R-and-B boy bands, I suppose.)

If the date were to involve movies—well, if there were a Robert De Niro film around, that's where Justin would want to go and buy Licorice Whips.

His favorite actress is Reese Witherspoon, so if you've got a Robert De Niro film with Reese in it, the concession stand had better be well stocked opening night!

One of the reasons that I find Justin so cool (besides his bravery with the dance steps and his love for jazz) is that he's not afraid to be seen in pictures wearing his glasses!

Yeah, sure, lots of times he's apparently wearing contacts, because he has put on shows and done videos without his glasses. Still, there are plenty of pictures with Justin wearing his specs—and they're not shades. He still looks fly—but he's also down to earth, too. Maybe he's just finished reading a history book or something in those pictures.

Maybe it's just me, but I like men in glasses.

Men in black with glasses, too!

Anyway, "down to earth" is definitely an apt phrase for Justin Paul Jeffre.

Let's push in the camera a bit and focus up a bit more on other aspects of the "deep-voiced guy."

GETTING DOWN WITH BIG J

Believe it or not, Justin at one time in his life was very, very shy.

You wouldn't think it. Not with his past in the performing arts. He certainly doesn't look shy in that high-school picture on the Web!

Nonetheless, Justin claims—and the others who have known him for a while all agree—that at one time he had difficulty speaking his mind, and certainly had a hard time talking with girls.

Now, though, he's changed.

Word has it that with realizing that he had lots to offer others, Justin has decided that he should live life to the fullest, and if he makes a goof of himself . . . well, so what?

Justin just wants to be himself.

And a worthy self it is, too.

Justin's goal in life is ". . . to be big enough where we can really have an impact on certain things. I always want to make a difference," he wanted everyone to know on the 98° home page.

"Justin is calm, cool and collected," Jeff says in the special 98° issue of *Pop Star*. "He's our wise man."

"He's very laid back," adds Nick, "which can help when things get stressful."

Indeed, Justin's rep is that he's the cool head of the bunch.

Once, when the power went out on a show and the guys had to sing *a cappella* for forty minutes, you can bet that Justin was the main force in keeping the panic down!

(You have to wonder if they sang their classic rendition of "The Star-Spangled Banner" at that show!)

But it's no secret either that Justin likes to party. Not being shy anymore must help him socialize. Rumor is that, being in New York now, club capital of the world, Justin just loves going out and making the scene. You have to think that with all the places the gang goes to sing now, Justin's getting a very good idea of what the insides of dance clubs all around the globe look like!

Practicing his dance steps?

Hopefully! But, most likely, just soaking up all the excitement and fun that cities have to offer.

The other guys also report that Justin's not shy about speaking his mind anymore. He'll tell you exactly what he thinks about everything—from who should be elected president in the year 2000 to what he thinks of the shoes you're wearing.

Justin's very brave, considering his past.

Apparently, he's been hurt a lot.

"I've had my heart broken so many times, I don't even know which one was the worst," Justin acknowledged to *BB* magazine. "I fall in love very easily." He must have snapped his fingers at that point in the interview. "It could happen like that."

Still, for as easily as he falls in love, Justin has managed to stay unentangled.

"We're all very, very single," he's said at one time. "I'm as single as you can get."

So. Here we have a young guy in his twenties. Sings bass and is pretty darned available. Likes to party. Has strong opinions and is quite willing to express them.

Right. And he can sing bass in a vocal group and harmonize like nobody's business.

Missing piece?

Well, clearly he's got a sense of humor and he's a focused guy. But let's just take a look at what he's written on the CDs that the group has released.

"I thank the Creator for making my dreams come true and blessing me in so many ways. Thank you Mom, Dad, Fran, Dan, Pam, Alexandra, Grandma, Stella, Aaron and the rest of my great big wonderful family. I couldn't have made it without the love and support you all have given me. To my friends Paul, Kamau, Chris, Sadie, (the one and only) Kirk, Lisa, Brad, Victor, Jon, Kip, Mike, Paris D'Jon, and Jonny '5.' SCPA and The Avenues crew, you know you have my love. Drew, Jeff, Nick—let's keep on bringing the funk. To all our fans around the world 98° love you."

Obviously, this is a guy with a close family and lots of friends. A good sign. He's a grateful fella. (There's lots of times he's told the press how grateful he is, how humbled by the group's success—and how they don't get big heads because they just keep on feeling blessed.)

But more than that, notice that he thanks the Creator.

Of course, all the different guys have different idea of how they relate to a Creator—but they all love God in their own ways. This isn't exactly Sunday-school music here (although I for one would love to see the guys light into some juicy, freewheeling gospel!)

Nonetheless, Just loves God, he loves his mom and dad, his relatives, his friends.

He's one wonderful guy.
And 98° fans!
Never, ever forget!
Baby, (chuckle) Justin loves you!

Fourth Degree: Drew Lachey

One of the first questions poor Drew always gets from interviewers goes something like this:

Hey Drew! Is it hard to be in a pop group with your older brother? Like, do you fight a lot, man, and do you have, like sibling rivalry and do you sometimes wanna kill each other?

Maybe that's what you're wondering, too? You probably would be if you had an older (or younger) brother hanging around all the time.

Still, Drew has no problem with that.

Usually he answers with something like he told *Popstar* magazine: No problem!

"I love sharing memories with him. Nick's my best friend. He's probably gonna be the best man at my wedding—"

Whoa! Does this mean that the youngest Degree is going to the first to get hitched? When . . . ?

Drew laughs at the thought. "No. (My wedding's) like 50 years down the line!"

Whew!

So, he'll be available for a while, at least.

Let's get some hard bio facts on the lad, shall we?

Andrew John Lachey was born August 8, 1976. You may have noticed that big brother Nick was born in Harlan, Kentucky. So, the Lachey clan must have made the move to Cincinnati somewhere between those years.

This gives us a chance to talk a little bit more about the city that three of the guys call home.

"It's one of the two bigger cities in Ohio," Drew told *Lime* magazine. "It's fairly conservative, but it's a great place to grow up. It's got a lot of beautiful forests, some pretty cold winters and pretty hot summers. I love it!"

Winston Churchill once described it as "The most beautiful of the inland cities of the union."

Actually, Drew was wrong. Cincinnati is actually the third largest city in Ohio, with Columbus and Akron coming before it . . . but it's probably the most famous! In the nineteenth century it was known as "Queen of the West" and the queen has kept up her appearance.

Cincinnati is the largest city on the Ohio River, though. It's in southwestern Ohio, sixteen miles east of the Indiana border. The place is a major manufacturing center, specializing in three products—R-and-B boy bands (strike that, just kidding) . . .

Music plays an important part in Cincinatti's heritage. It has an excellent symphony orchestra, and plenty of singing organizations.

This must have gotten into Drew Lachey's blood.

He spent a lot of time with singer Nick as he was growing up—they had their own secret clubhouse together and they probably listened to records and sang.

Despite his serious face, he's always been considered the comedian of the family.

Drew loves his pictures—he takes a lot of them—and they stretch all the way back to his childhood. "I love having memories," he told the Asian magazine *Teen Trends*. Some of his favorite memories, he also told that magazine, were: "Trips that my grandparents used to take us on. We would pile into their motor home and just go all over."

Like Justin and Nick, Drew also went to the School for Creative and Performing Arts, but he started a little younger than they did. He was accepted into that school when he was in the fifth grade, getting perfect scores on his application tests.

As he was growing up, his vocal talents did not go unnoticed. Not only did he work with the Cincinnati Opera on a few shows, but he also appeared in a famous ballet.

Drew is also quite an outdoorsy sort of guy. One of his full summer vacations was spent working at a Wyoming ranch owned by his aunt. Later, he went on to become a camp counselor.

Although he did not go to college, he did a stint in the army. Then, Drew went on to become an ambulance driver and emergency medical technician in Brooklyn, New York.

Drew once used his EMT training to help a woman on a plane that the group was on—and he almost had to use it in a strange situation while the group was on tour:

"We were driving on 15N," he told *Teen Trends* magazine. "When we saw an overturned car laying in the median and someone was pulling something out of the car. We thought it was a person. We pulled over to help and he was just pulling out a purse. Everyone was alright, just scratches. But for that split second that we didn't know it was very intense."

He wasn't sorry to leave full-time livesaving, though.

"I was an ambulance driver in New York, which was kind of stressful," he told *Big UK* magazine. "So when my brother called me and asked me to join the group I packed a case, closed my bank account and ran."

It must have taken a lot of work learning the songs he started singing with 98°. And his experience singing with groups and in shows must have helped quite a bit as he started singing around with them.

When asked by *Big UK* what the funniest thing that ever happened to him, he had to respond: "It wasn't funny at the time but I arrived in Los Angeles to join the band and they told me that we were supporting Montell Jordan the next night. I cried with panic."

Still, although he was the last to join, Drew had to put in his time at jobs to support their efforts.

For a while he worked the midnight shift at a deli to make ends meet.

Drew's favorite car is a BMW M3.

Hope he's driving one now, but he's probably too busy promoting the new album to buy one.

But what exactly is Drew like, in person?

I won't keep you in suspense long.

GETTING CLOSE TO DREW

The other guys in the band used to call him "Radar" because he reminded them of the character on *MASH*.

Now they call him "Sprout."

Why?

"Because I'm a midget," Drew told *Popstar* magazine.

Hmm. Let's look at the stats.

Andrew John Lachey.

Height: Five foot six inches.

That's not a midget! That's not that short, either! Next to Michael Jordan maybe—

But five-and-a-half-feet tall is a perfect size, really.

Maybe Drew feels bad about it, though. It's true that lots of girls are getting taller and taller, and it's also true that many women like men to be taller than they are.

If Drew called you up for a date, would you turn him down because he's too short?

If you think you might, you'd better think again, because if he's not exactly as tall as the other 98° guys, you can be sure he's all heart.

Check this fact out:

Drew misses being at home in Cincinnati.

"Me and Nick have a six-year-old little brother," he also told *Popstar*. "We came back just a couple of days ago after seven months. It's amazing how much he's grown and matured."

Drew obviously cares about family and people . . .

He's sweet and funny and self-deprecating.

Okay, okay—so Jeff's got the muscles and Nick's got the drop-dead gorgeous model looks, and Justin's got that deep Voice—Drew's got plenty going for him.

Listen up!

SOME TIME WITH DREW

So 98° has come to sing in your town.

There's a contest the local radio station is doing. It's like this: Write down three 98° songs on a card with your name and phone number.

What would you choose!

(Hint: Pick "True to your Heart," "Heat It Up" and "Invisible Man.")

You win!

Each of the four winners gets a chance to have a burger and fries at the local fifties hangout with one of the group.

You get Drew!

That night, the concert is awesome. The guys just sing their hearts out. They dance really well and they shake lots of hands. The music is really sweet and exciting, and the lights are spectacular, the beat is intense and the heat . . .

Whew!

You're heart is pounding with excitement.

You get to spend some time with one of them! Andrew, the guy with those fine, fine, baritone pipes!

There's a cool stretch limo waiting for you and you get ushered to the fifties-style joint (you know, with malts and ice cream and booths and stools that play the old-style music that the 98° loves so much).

So, you get shown to your booth.

You order a chocolate ice cream shake and you sip it.

Here comes Drew!

He's still a little damp from the shower he took (boy, those lights must have been hot! He was sweating like crazy up there on the stage!), but his eyes are bright and he's got this big, big smile on. And he's even cuter in person than he is on stage or in those pictures.

He smells good, too, as he slides into the booth beside you—and you can just tell that he's full of life and love and sexy stuff and . . .

"Hi," he says.

You say, "Hi, Andy!"

His smile turns into a frown.

He looks upset.

Yikes! You forgot to read the whole book!

DREW STUFF

If you ever get to hang with Drew Lachey, there's one thing you should know.

Never, ever call him Andy!

Drew is one focused guy.

It's one of his many amazing talents and qualities and a hallmark of his character. "Drew represents the organization of 98°," his big brother Nick points out. "He's the one who makes sure we're all on the same page of the music and that we're all organized."

Where did he get this skill?

Remember that Drew used to be an emergency medical technician.

He's said that this job (as singer, group member, hat tree and heart-throb) isn't as stressful as driving ambulances and saving people's lives, but it must get hairy sometimes, and it sure must help to have had the experience.

In fact, once it literally did!

Drew and the guys were on an airplane, headed for a tour. One of the passengers had a heart attack.

It was Drew who knew what to do to save his life . . . and he just jumped right in and did it.

Drew's a hero in other ways.

You remember how the guys hooked up with Paris D'Jon as their manager and they got the gig opening for Montell Jordan? Well, when Drew accepted the job and drove out with his brother Nick all the way from the east coast, he had to learn all his vocal parts from Nick and from tapes in the car—on the way. There was barely time to practice. Nonetheless, despite all this, the guys did so well at that gig that this was when they started generating that label buzz.

Although he's got a sweet and open face, don't let that fool you. Nick's a real comic—and always has been the comedian of the family.

With the hectic 98° schedule, it must be a relief to have a guy around, cracking jokes all the time.

As though you haven't guessed by now, Nick is also a keen fan of baseball caps. He's got a huge collection, and it's very rarely (like maybe he's posing for a glamor shot) that you don't see him with one on.

Backward!

What's with the backward cap?

Well, yeah, the Beastie Boys have done that for a long time, and, of course, with rap groups it's de rigueur.

Me, I say, Drew's out to get a new image!

Try the cap on the other way around once in a while, Drew!

At the very least it will keep the sun out of your eyes!

Anyway, from the cap thing you'd think that Drew would be into baseball, mostly. Although there's no indication he doesn't like baseball, when pressed, the sports that he'll enthuse about are snowboarding and water skiing.

These are definitely participatory sports, so I assume that, in the summer, when the group isn't working hard in the studio, Drew goes out and kicks up some water spume for fun. Conversely, in the winter, he probably heads for the slopes.

For sit-down-and-relax-type sports, Drew prefers football. He'll sit and drink his favorite, orange juice, and scarf up all kinds of junk food. He especially adores pizza and patries. And doughnuts! Forget about it!

Girls—if you want to get Drew's attention, don't wave panties or bras or wink or anything like that—just hold up a big box of fresh Dunkin' Donuts, assorted flavors!

DETAILS, DETAILS

So, after a snack of doughnuts, Drew might get into his Tommy Hilfiger clothing (his fave duds) and start thinking about his next vacation.

Where, oh where, would he like to go?

Well, chances are, out of the city. Drew is the one guy of the bunch who's not super, super thrilled about visiting cities. Oh, he probably enjoys the excitement and the challenge— but, at heart, he prefers peace and quiet.

What Drew would be dreaming about in those Tommy Hilfiger pants, that Tommy Hilfiger shirt, that Tommy Hilfiger cap (on backwards) would be some time in a cabin, way way out in the mountains and woods, probably by a burbling brook, among pine smells and flower tastes, and with a nice big stereo to play his favorite music when he's tired of listening to crickets and burblings.

And what would the brown-haired, hazel-eyed cutie be listening to?

Well, R and B, of course.

But, you know, Drew doesn't listen to just R and B.

When *Popstar* magazine asked him what CD in his music collection would surprise his fans the most, Drew answered,

"CD of Samuel Barber. He's an American composer who has a string piece 'Adagio for Strings' that's one of my favorite music works ever."

Of course, being a guy, he probably also likes straight rock, but let's take a closer look at what he'd be putting on his portable boombox to sweeten that country air during a restful vacation.

Well, there would be lots of Marvin Gaye.

And what's this? Oodles of Prince CDs (oops, sorry . . . the Artist formerly known as Prince, or as some wags today call him, the Artist Formerly Known).

In fact, Drew says his favorite song of all time is Prince's "Purple Rain."

Also, there'd be lots of that inspiration for the whole group, Take 6, to play.

(You can check out the pieces on all these groups later on. Do! Great stuff!)

Of course, if you pressed him for travel possibilities outside the U.S., Drew would admit that he does have a couple of wish destinations in mind, namely South America and the Bahamas.

Beach spots.

"It's that nice-weather thing," Drew explains.

But here's a thought.

Whether he's out for some fresh country air and some peace and quiet, or off to an exotic beach with tranquil breakers lapping and the smell of sand and suntan lotion, what kind of girl would Drew most like to be his companion on such a trip?

GIRL OF DREW'S DREAMS

You're at the beach.

It's not just any beach, but a place of beautiful white sand that stretches off into stands of exotic palm trees. A gentle and balmy breeze caresses you as you lie on the beach towel, a glass of ice-cold fruit juice tinkling in your hand. The smell of coconut oil is in the air, only it's not from the trees—it's from your expensive bottle of sun-tan lotion.

The water is crystal clear and inviting and you can't wait until your companion comes back from the cabana so that you can go out and swim with him.

Here he comes. He's so cute! He's got long black baggy swimming pants that ride his slender waist. He's in good shape, too, and he's carrying a great big boombox that's blasting Take 6 doing a fabulous version of "Biggest Part of Me."

He's got a cap and it's on backward.

It's Drew Lachey of 98°.

What kind of girl are you?

Well . . . actually, you could be anyone!

"I like a girl that is adventurous and likes to try new things. They don't have to be a particular type—I'm open for whatever," Drew told an AOL chat.

Actually, on Canadian TV, he got a little more specific.

"When I look for a girl, I look for a girl that just loves life, likes having a good time, likes having fun."

Turns out, though, that there is a type he likes.

The sporty type.

So if you're into snorkeling or skiing—Drew would like that very much, there on the beautiful Bermuda beach.

In fact, this is just the sort of thing he enjoys doing on dates, to get to know girls.

"I'm more the outdoor type, so I'd like to go horseback riding or something. I like my girls active, athletic, so, something like that."

Why?

Because it's kind of an icebreaker. It's a way that Drew—probably very shy despite his jokey demeanor—can be with a girl without feeling too awkward.

Then, as they share splashes in the water or spills on the slope (complete with laughter and thrills), he can open up more to a girl, and be himself.

And if you were around Drew when he opened up more—exactly what would you find?

INSIDE DREW

A telling thing happened on TV recently that shed quite a bit of light on Drew's character, and his place in 98°.

The show was *Loveline*. It's kind of talk radio—only on TV. You've got a couple of clever TV personalities, plus a therapist, plus guests. Oh yes, an audience . . .

Viewers call in and talk about their, um, relationship problems, with a heavy emphasis on the physical side of those relationships.

On one show, 98° were the guests.

They got a lot of their current video shown and they did some *a cappella* singing

Then they chipped in and gave their thoughts about whatever problem was being discussed.

What was quite fascinating was that while the other guys just sat back on the couch, looking at ease and casual, but engaged—Drew was sitting right on the edge of his couch, absolute and totally excited, together and focused.

You can't help but think that this is the way he is in the group's life. Up early, on the phone, doing business, making sure that everything goes right . . .

Or in the studio, making sure that he knows exactly what he has to contribute to make the song that's being produced just exactly right . . .

Or at the concert, making sure that the fans get just the best show possible . . .

Every single time.

Intense!

That's the word you might use of Drew. He's intensely funny, intensely talented and intensely committed to the goals of 98°.

"Drew is the guy who's must concerned about business and taking care of that," says Justin in *Pop Star*.

Well, we're not talking about Elvis-style "taking care of business," a phrase the 'King of Rock n' Roll' made rather obnoxious.

And we're not just talking about selling t-shirts or temporary tattoos, either.

We're talking about the whole serious aspect of everything that makes 98° go . . .

But what's beneath the neat socks and underwear in the drawer and his other organized ways?

Let's look at what Drew wrote in his liner notes for the latest album to get some kind of insight:

"First I would like to thank God for His never-ending blessing. Lea-LDDL. Pops, Iris, Ike for their love and prayers. Mom, Jeff and the Rugrats for the support. The Top 40 family—Fred Gargamel and Angela. The ever-expanding Garret clan, Jason, a.k.a. Larry. The Lachey, Fopma, Leimach and Staley families and of course Hydro, Sugar and Hollywood— Let's make it count!'

There you have Drew's priorities.

God.

Family.

Making it count.

Drew Lachey is very concerned about the impact the group has not just on music, but on lives.

He wants the group's music to bring people together, and he wants to use their example—and their charity work—to help make the world a better place.

Drew is definitely someone worth listening to—whether it's singing or speaking.

Vocal Groups

First Tenor. Second Tenor. Baritone. Bass.

There's nothing quite like it. The rich vibrations of four male voices locked into complex and shifting harmonies, the high, startling first tenor soaring with the melody while a deep and thumping bass voice shivers the hairs on your toes.

All without any musical instruments to dilute the purity.

98°, although a ballad band supreme, and a group that can whip up a dance number as well as anyone, are primarily a vocal group, a harmony group, and they come from a long tradition that they are proud to acknowledge. One of the things that make Jeff, Nick, Drew and Justin unique in the pop-music world today is just how well they carry the torch of four-part male harmony singers.

As good as CDs and stereo equipment are these days, trust me—there's nothing like being in the same room with a fine singer. Four great singers, harmonizing—it's a wonderful experience. Recently, when 98° did their famous *a cappella* interpretation of "She's Out of My Life" on MTV's *Total Request,* you can see the sweet human effect this kind of vocal work has on people—the camera panned across the reactions of the teenage girls in the audience and it was clear they were having a warm and astonishing experience.

Four-part male harmony singing is the cornerstone of the 98° experience. Let's take a closer look at exactly what it is, and where it came from.

*   *   *

Full choirs, of course, have four basic parts. Women sing soprano or alto. Men sing tenor or bass.

Four-part groups are like a small choir, with men doing the high parts. (Sometimes—like with Smokey Robinson or the Bee Gees, male voices can literally get as high as women's—but it's a vocal trick known as *falsetto*, which, unless done properly, sounds pretty silly). There of course are four-part harmony groups like Manhattan Transfer, with women doing the high parts.

Jeff Timmons and Nick Lachey mostly trade their matinee idol leads (with Drew coming in some times as well as sing lead) when they croon, but when the guys blend their voices, it's Jeff as first tenor who generally takes the lead, with Nick doing harmony. As baritone Drew Lachey's job is to keep the lower parts steady—as Justin Jeffre pounds out the deep and resounding notes that give the total such power and resonance.

One of the earliest forms of this sort of singing became popular in America over a century ago and is still being practiced. This is the barbershop quartet. Justin and Nick belong to a barbershop quartet that's been singing off and on since high school. Barbershop quartets from all over the world come together to sing for audiences—and each other—keeping up this wonderful tradition. (Although it's a primarily male avocation, there are at least two organizations of women barbershop singers—Sweet Adelines and Harmony Incorporated.) The main organization is The Society for The Preservation and Encouragement of Barber Shop Quartet Singing in America.

The style got its start as far back as England in the the time of Shakespeare. Men waiting at the barbership for a trim—or perhaps even the letting of blood—passed the time by harmonizing together on popular songs. This tradition was revived in the old American West, and soon the style truly became popular from about 1895 to 1930.

This was also about the time when jazz was becoming more and more popular. It could be argued that it was groups of black men who carried on the tradition of close harmony singing that led to 98°. Two of the most popular of these were the Mills Brother and the Ink Spots.

The Mills Brothers were formed in 1925 in Piqua, Ohio (Ohioans just like our guys!). They called themselves "Four Boys and a Kazoo" but, although they had an instrument, it was their voices that gained them popularity. These voices blended together in a harmony so tightly because they were brothers, certainly—but they weren't just doing harmonies . . . they were swinging those harmonies in a jazzy kind of way. Before they became the Mills Brothers, they were also "Four Boys and a Guitar." When one of the brothers died in 1936, their father stepped in and they created such hits as "Glow Worm" "Paper Doll" and "Up a Lazy River."

The next step toward 98° was The Ink Spots. These were black artists as well and while they had great harmony, they were known for featuring soloists on pop songs such as "My Prayer," "When the Swallows Come Back to Capistrano" and "Don't Get Around Much Anymore" while the other members sang sweet "ooohs" and "ahhhs" as backup. The Ink Spots had their heyday in the forties, but they created a sound that influenced many, many groups in the early part of the fifties.

When Nick sang "In the Still of the Night" to that secretary, and when 98° do the first part of their *a cappella* arrangement of "She's Out of My Life," the guys show how well they know doo-wop music.

Nick and Justin also fool around with a doo-wop group called The Avenues, and have since high school.

Doo wop was named after the nonsense syllables these groups of the fifties and sixties used to back up their lead. The first doo-wop group is generally thought to be The Orioles, who spawned many groups named after birds, such as the Larks and the Flamingoes. Doo-wop singing was something that guys in urban neighborhoods could do and be cool—it's street music in the way that rap is. You don't need instruments, just voices and time and practice. Doo-wop was a part of the rhythm-and-blues craze of the mid-fifties, and continued to develope with black artists such as the Platters, the Cleftones and the Coasters, Frankie Lymon and the Teen-agers and many more . . . It didn't take long for white groups to start imitating the style, resulting in the Capris, Danny and the Juniors and Dion and the Belmonts. However, 98° prob-ably swings more toward their black forebears in style, even though they can "sh'boom" and "sha la la" with the best of them.

The group that probably was the most influential in the doo-wop period in terms of R-and-B development was The Drifters. At first with Clyde McPhatter on lead and then with Ben E. King, these folks produced such great songs as "Money Honey," "There Goes My Baby" and "This Magic Moment," and many more.

But a group that was probably more influential on the style that 98° came to perfect were the Platters. This group, like 98°, specialized in killer romantic ballads such as "The Great Pretender" and "Only You."

The doo-wop groups influenced the generations that fol-lowed, including Boyz II Men. But one of the many won-derful things about 98° is that you can see how they've heard all this music and incorporpated it all into a unique vocal sound not only of today, but echoing the best vocal groups of the past.

You can get any of the groups mentioned here on CD.

Tell the store owner that 98° sent you!

Motown

When you say "Motown Records" the tendency is to think of great songs, classic soul. Now, of course, that label's really big act is Boyz II Men, but look (and listen) back to the sixties and seventies and it's pretty staggering to think about all the great groups that have been on that record label. Let's drop a few names, shall we?

Diana Ross and the Supremes. The Temptations. Smokey Robinson and the Miracles. The Four Tops. The Jackson Five. Stevie Wonder. Martha and the Vandellas. The Marvellettes. Marvin Gaye. The list goes on and on.

And now, of course, Motown has 98° to carry on the tradition of greatness.

Jeff, Nick, Justin and Drew are well aware of this heritage. In fact, they've been doing Temptations songs since well before they were signed. Early shows featured a Temptin' Temptations tribute medley, and even now the guys just love to sing an incredibly accurate version of "I Can't Get Next To You."

A book that talked about 98° and R and B in general that did not mention a little of the history of Motown—well, it wouldn't be doing its job!

Motown, of course, wasn't just the music that Murphy Brown liked to dance around to in her well-known sitcom.

Motown Records was the work of a man named Berry Gordy, Jr.

In the fifties, Berry Gordy, a black man, wrote songs for a big act of the time, Jackie Wilson. But Gordy had a dream of greater success . . . a record label of his own. A company owned by a black man that would feature mostly black artists—and sell the American public on black music and artistry with the style of hard work he saw Jackie Wilson give in his shows.

In 1959, with a mere eight hundred dollars borrowed from his family, Berry Gordy, Jr. started Motown Records. Motown because that was the nickname of the Motor City, namely, Detroit, Michigan.

One of the first artists released on this brand-new label was Barrett Strong, whose 1960 song, "Money (That's What I Want" was later covered by The Beatles. This was co-written by Gordy, who also did much of the early songwriting. However, as money indeed poured in and Motown began styling itself as "The Sound of Young America," Berry's label acquired more artists and songwriters.

Sometimes, the artists themselves—like Little Stevie Wonder, Smokey Robinson and Marvin Gaye were also writers, like 98°. But much of the music was penned by professional songwriters, a tradition which is still in vogue in much of R and B (and country music) today. Throughout it all, Berry Gordy kept a strong grip on the creative proceedings, and made sure his artists were well dressed and performed with sharp professionalism.

One of the achievements of Motown was its breaking out of the R-and-B charts and into the mainstream charts. Berry succeeded at this by wedding the styles and passion of R and B and gospel with simple, hummable melodies that simply will be around as long as there are people to hum them. This approach can certainly be seen in 98°. A ballad simply won't go anywhere without a good melody, and the guys excel at ballads.

Back to the sixties, though.

It could be stated fairly that without Motown, much of the great pop music of the '60s would have been British. Some of the great girl groups (as opposed to today's boy bands) were Motowners. These included the Marvelettes, Martha and the Vandellas and, of course, the immortal Supremes. At this time, the emphasis was not so much on harmony as the call-and-response relationship with the lead singer (with the Supremes, of course, that would be Diana Ross). Although they are known for their harmony, this is still the case to some extent with 98°.

One of the biggest stars and creative talents behind the Motown success was William "Smokey" Robinson, who wrote songs for Motown, as well as recording them with his vocal group, The Miracles. Robinson's sweet and true falsetto soared above his songs, most memorably "Tears of a Clown," and set the standard for smooth, high R-and-B voices. His song "My Guy" as performed by Mary Wells was Motown's first number-one pop hit, and "My Girl," another Robinson song, was the biggest-selling single for Motown and the group that performed it, The Temptations. He's still going strong now.

Speaking of the Temptations, they were the Backstreet Boys of their day—and thanks to the resurgence of interest in their music (a two-part TV miniseries told their story recently) they'll be around for a lot longer under their current grouping. (Well-known Temps Eddie Kendricks and David Ruffin died a few years ago, and two other members have gone to the great gospel choir in the sky.) They sang a lot of great songs supremely well, and had unforgettable dance routines to go along with the music, which included fabulous songs including "Just My Imagination," "I Wish it Would Rain" and "Cloud Nine."

My favorite Motown guy group has to be the Four Tops—a bunch who, like 98°, danced around a bit, but mostly relied on great vocal blend, great songs—and powerhouse singing—to get across their tunes. Of course, the Four Tops are not particularly smooth like the Degrees, but with songs like "Bernadette" "Reach Out" and "Baby I Need Your Loving" to belt, they don't need to be. The Four Tops—without one of their members, Lawrence Payton, who died in 1997—

are now three and perform as The Tops. Soul at its zenith, in my opinion.

The Four Tops did three collaboration albums with the Supremes. If there is one group from Motown's classic heyday that had the most hits, it was the Supremes. If 98° can rack up as many great, great songs as the Supremes did, they will be lucky indeed. "Baby Love," "Stop in the Name of Love," "You Keep Me Hanging On" . . . the hits just kept on coming from this group, helping Motown to get another nickname—"Hitsville U.S.A." Diana Ross left in 1969 for a distinguished solo career, but the Supremes soldier on, led by Mary Wilson, who was with them from the beginning.

Marvin Gaye was a classic soul singer and excellent writer whose work, even now, is echoed in groups like 98°. He is quoted as saying "I never wanted to shake my ass—I just wanted to sit on a stool and sing sweet love songs" (just like Nick and Jeff). However, Gaye's not remembered for his sweet songs, but rather for his smouldering and emotional stuff. This, of course, is where pop—music created basically to divert and entertain—gets way deep and closer to art, although to be good pop, like 98°, it has to be at least artful. Marvin Gaye, like many other soul and R-and-B artists, had roots in gospel. He died in 1984, and is one of the most-mourned singers who died young.

Some people think that 98° is the Motown's first white band. Far from the truth! One of the major white acts from Motown was Rare Earth, a rock-and-soul act who signed with Motown in 1968 and did a great version of The Temptations "Get Ready." A bigger band than most, these guys put some horns and crunch into the soul mix, sounding a little like a Motown Blood, Sweat and Tears with a healthy dollop of psychedelic sound sometimes in the mix. One of their best songs "I Just Want to Celebrate" is still a classic, heard all the time on classic rock radio, and still played by the band itself, which puts on a spunky, sassy show that is particularly popular in Europe.

Finally, whenever mentioning early Motown, it would be impossible to ignore the Jackson Five. As teenagers trained by their father, Joe Jackson, Jackie Jackson, Tito Jackson, Marlon Jacksonand the very young Michael—absolutely put sass and excitement into pop music that gave Motown a real shot in the arm. Their hits—which include "ABC," "The Love You Save" and "I Want You Back" are prototypes for the energy needed by pop groups.

Later, Randy Jackson, Latoya Jackson and Janet Jackson joined the group. But, of course, it was Michael and Janet who have proved to be enduring stars (alas, on other labels). Still, Motown found them, groomed them and launched them—and thus altered the music scene. Talk about original boy bands!

In the mid-seventies to early eighties, Lionel Richie and the Commodores were just about Motown's only success story. Gordy's move to L.A. brought some worthwhile movies such as *Lady Sings the Blues* and *The Wiz* into being, but the label lost many of its big stars such as Diana Ross. In 1988, Berry Gordy sold the label, but kept his hand in the creative process somewhat.

In the 1990s though, Motown is Hitsville again. Under the excellent guidance of Andre Harrell, its work with such stars as Queen Latifah, Horace Brown, Montel Jordan, Johnny Gill, Boyz II Men and, of course, 98° has made it a star in contemporary music again.

Now, there's a popular chain of restaurants called the Motown Cafe, which you can bet will always be filled with good music. Motown has a special night on MTV, and its own hot variety show, which, hopefully, will feature 98° soon.

The label, of course, still keeps many of the great older artists in its catalog in print for new generations to discover.

If you don't have any classic Motown records, a really good place to start would be their incredible collection *Hitsville USA—The Motown Singles Collection 1959–1971*. This four-CD collection has 104 songs by 36 artists . . . and lots more information about this era in music in a nice book filled with pictures. There's also a second collection from the seventies of fine songs, but the first collection is the most essential, with all the artists mentioned in this section represented with their biggest hits, their best music of that time.

I think that the members of 98° would agree with me on this one: For R-and-B fans, this one's a must!

Motown Forever!

Other Great Groups

I hope you got something out of those all-too-brief histories of vocal groups and Motown. The music is rich and wonderful.

If you like what 98° does, but aren't too familiar with some of the groups I've mentioned in this book, here's a little background material to get your started.

I dare you to keep your toes from tapping, your head from nodding and your soul from rejoicing when you hear this music!

BOYZ II MEN

Remember those guys we mentioned, who 98° tried to get in to see backstage at their L.A. concert?

That's right. Boyz II Men.

Well, these guys are just the best.

One of the interesting things is that two of the four members are brothers, too. That would be Wanya and Nathan Morris. They and Shawn Stockman and Mike McCary, buddies who could carry a tune, harmonize and who thought that R and B should also mean rich and blissful, got together and practiced in Philadelphia. They all attended that city's High School for Creative and Performing Arts.

After being discovered in 1990, they produced their first album, an amazing record called *Cooleyhighharmony*. Not only did the album reach the million-seller mark that would make it a platinum record, it soared past that mark, selling about nine million units.

What the Boyz had was harmony, as well as soul and melody, the hit singles from the album just kept on coming from "It's So Hard to Say Goodbye to Yesterday," "Please Don't Go," "Uh, Ah" and their absolute classic "Motown Philly."

With Shawn and Wanya the tenors, Nathan on baritone and Shawn on bass, the hits just continued, including "End of the Road" and "I'll Make Love to You."

They've got other CDs out there, including *CD II*, a Christmas album and *Evolution*.

The thing about Boyz II Men, besides their incredible weavings of voices and their rich harmonies is their sincerity. Like 98°, their faith in God is very important to them, and they're happy to credit love and their Maker as top priorities in their lives.

Trust me. If you like 98°, don't go out and buy 'N Sync. Get the real stuff.

Get Boy's II Men.

Cooleyhighharmony is a good place to start.

STEVIE WONDER

You get a teensy taste of Stevie Wonder with the song "True to Your Heart," but there's a heck of a lot more to the man than a harmonica and a distinctive voice. That's why I think that 98° would point to him as an artist to look into for more great, great R and B.

Stevie Wonder is the name that Berry Gordy gave a young man whose given name was Steveland Morris. When Wonder started out with Motown at the tender age of eleven, he was dubbed "Little" Stevie Wonder, and his first big hit was "Fingertips Part Two." After a number of songs, his voice changed and his talents sharpened even more—and he was responsible for a huge number of hits for Motown—

including "Uptight (Everything's Alright)" and a fine version of Bob Dylan's "Blowin' in the Wind." He worked with other artists and wrote songs that include one of my favorites, "Tears of a Clown," which Smokey Robinson and the Miracles made famous.

It was in the seventies, though, that Wonder, long past the "Little," really made the albums that declared his genius. After getting control of his music and how he wanted to present it, Stevie Wonder was responsible for a number of albums that became popular with everyone, in every kind of music, blending R and B with rock, African music with reggae and classical . . . gosh, they just have everything, encased in unforgettable melodies and lyrics. "Superstition," "You Are the Sunshine of My Life," "Living for the City," "Higher Ground" and many more are now staples of musical life. Moreover, his work with new kinds of instruments (he was one of the first black artists to use synthesizers, for instance), and his innovations, did nothing less than to enlarge the scope of R and B—making it the kind of music that 98° sings now.

Stevie Wonder was also extremely active in working on black identity in America, a theme which often surfaces in his music. For instance, his tireless efforts were effective in making Martin Luther King's birthday a national holiday.

It would be hard to pick a single album to recommend starting with, but probably the best two to get a sampling of Stevie Wonder's work are *Greatest Hits I*, which covers his work up to 1968, *Greatest Hits II*, which goes up to 1972 and, finally, *Original Musiquarium I*, which samples his songs up to 1982.

You can't go wrong with any of these.

One of my favorites of Wonder's is the much more recent *Conversation Peace*, which critics didn't give super-great reviews, but I think is just fine, thank you, with really tuneful songs, soulful playing and singing—and heartfelt themes.

Stevie Wonder has always had a reputation for helping worthy new artists out. With "True to Your Heart," he gave 98° a great boost.

If you're a 98° fan, and aren't much aware of Stevie Wonder—well, I think that Jeff, Nick, Justin and Drew would just slap their foreheads, roll their eyes and say, "Hey! Head for the record store!"

TAKE 6

If there's one contemporary group that 98°—and any R-and-B harmony group—aspires to become like, it's Take 6.

Why?

Well, this group comes up from gospel roots. Their first recordings were *entirely a cappella*. And yet they had enough contemporary pizzazz to win millions of fans and influence many groups, including the important Boyz II Men.

Of all the younger groups that specialize in *a cappella*, in my opinion these guys are the very best. They've got vocal and spiritual integrity as well, and are equally popular on the gospel and Christian music scenes.

When Jeff Timmons went to see them in Ohio, they were so nice and encouraging that he kept that encouragment in mind when he went off to L.A. to search for fame and success as a member of a harmony group. Now, the members of 98° always pay tribute to Take 6 when they talk about music that's influenced them.

An no wonder.

Take 6 was formed at Oakwood College in Georgia. Gospel was the first expression of their amazingly tight and assured harmonies, but they've gone on to influence everyone in the R-and-B field, and have helped focus worldwide attention on *a cappella* singing.

If you find that you really like the last cut on *98° and Rising*, you should go and get the first or second Take 6 CDs, *Take 6* or *So Much to Say*. But, if you like a mix, and enjoy instruments as well, you get it all on the very easy to like *Join the Band* from 1994, which has everything, including a good song with R-and-B legend Ray Charles, "My Friend."

98° would probably say you should get them all, but I'd

say go with *Join the Band* first. It won a Grammy Award and, by the time you get to the last cut, a stirring "Lullaby," you'll only be able to agree with that pretigious award.

JAMES BROWN

After 98° were lucky enough to get Paris D'Jon as manager, they actually got a chance to open a gig for one of their idols. Justin Jeffre was particularly overwhelmed at the honor, and for good reason.

Along with Ray Charles, James Brown is perhaps the person most responsible for bridging modern R and B with classic gospel. In fact, he, like Charles, took much of his passion and stirring beats, his preacher's cadences from gospel and black tradition—and put them into searing mainstream.

"Soul was created by James Brown—gospel overtones with jazz licks," Brown has said.

Although Brown's music certainly is never particularly as smooth and flowing as 98° in their crooning mode, their dance tunes have some of Brown's flair. However, James Brown simply influenced all of R and B so much that, simply by being R and B artists, 98° owe him a debt. In the pressure cooker of his band—always filled with top-notch musicians— the R-and-B form known as *funk* was literally created. Funk, of course, tumbled into disco. It could even be said that Brown's music, particularly that of the sixties and the early seventies, helped created hip-hop and rap.

There's lots of stuff out there by James Brown, some of it okay . . . lots of it great. For example, most critics, when citing the best live performances on record, include James Brown's *Live at the Apollo*, from a show at that Harlem theater in 1962. This was the record that got him a lot of attention and fame. Soon James Brown started to be known as "The Hardest Working Man in Showbiz" and "The Godfather of Soul," names he created for himself.

There are huge, expensive collections of Brown's work, including *Star Time* (four discs) and lots of others, including some with his original group, The Famous Flames.

But a really good starter would be the special collection *James Brown—Greatest Hits*, a recent release from Poly-Gram. Inexpensive and short, but way hot, it's got the famous *Papa's Got a Brand New Bag, Pt. 1*, as well as other great pieces.

If you're not familiar with James Brown, and you're starting to like the kind of music that 98° do, try him.

Justin will be thrilled to think he helped turn you on to this great musician and soulful artist.

PRINCE

This guy used to be all over the radio, but now it's harder to find his music. This is mostly his own fault, but with 1999 all around (one of Prince's most popular songs is called "1999"), there's bound to be a revival.

Nick Lachey is a particular fan of Prince, and he probably wants you to listen to the guy's stuff, so pay close attention if you're not familiar with this performer.

Part of the problem is that Prince is officially no longer Prince. Prince Nelson Rogers, born June 7, 1958 in Minneapolis, is now known as "The Artist Formerly Known as Prince." "The Artist" uses a symbol that looks like something from an Egyptian tomb.

Whatever. His best albums are under the name Prince, and you can get them anywhere, so we'll call him Prince here.

Although he started out solidly soul and R and B, Prince made his mark by combining lots of other musical forms—such as rock, pop, jazz, gospel and world music—into a marvelous and potent brew all his own. With such songs as "Little Red Corvette" and "1999" he carved his way onto the charts and national consciousness. These were simply an introduction to what he was about to accomplish with the album of songs from his movie *Purple Rain*.

The songs "When Doves Cry," "Let's Go Crazy" and Nick's favorite, "Purple Rain" itself, all went high into the pop top ten, and Prince's tour afterward made him the pop/ R and B star of the eighties. Prince can play just about any instrument, and he did just that on *Purple Rain*, but it's his stirring guitar work, obviously influenced by that other black blues/rock deity Jimi Hendrix, that simply sewed all his sound into a sexy, jumping stew of brilliance.

Prince went on to other terrific albums including *Sign 'O' the Times* and *Parade (Music from the Motion Picture* Under the Cherry Moon*)* and he was responsible for some definitive songs covered by other artists including Sheena Easton and Sinead O'Connor, but his music output in the nineties was vast and diffuse and often unfocused.

Pay that no mind. If you ever get a chance to see Prince live, go for it. There is simply no more exciting R-and-B show going today. This is a man of vast talent and ability who still succeeds in inspiring artists like 98° to greater and greater heights.

What to buy? Well, all the albums above are brilliant, and nothing quite like anything else, R and B or rock included.

But if you were to choose one to start off, then Nick Lachey would probably point to *Music from Purple Rain* by Prince and the Revolution.

There isn't a bad song on the CD, and most are downright inspiring.

Of any artist in the R-and-B camp, Prince is probably the guy who best blends rock ideas into his music.

I predict that soon he'll take up the mantle again and lead both forms of music into the twenty-first century.

And maybe he'll call up 98° for some harmony work!

MONTELL JORDAN

If 98° were influenced by a whole distinguished group of performers, then one guy must stand out as the principal singer who influenced them personally. That, of course, is Montell Jordan, another Motown recording artist, whose soul-

ful voice and six feet, eight inches aren't all that have kept
him looming in the R-and-B field.

Jordan likes his sensitive love songs with a funky groove,
and he's probably most influenced vocally by folks like
Teddy Pendergrass, Luther Vandross, and, of course, the eternal Marvin Gaye. But what has put Jordan way up in the R-
and-B lover-guy ranks has been his understanding of current
production style and technique. If some singers prefer to hang
with the pretty girls, Jordan clearly has spent fruitful time
with R-and-B producers.

He's passed his knowledge on to 98°, probably during the
tour they went on together, and the time he worked with them
on a couple of songs for their first album. You can just imagine him saying, "No, no, Nick. More soul—less Eddie Ved-
der!"

The marvelous Paris D'Jon was one of Montell Jordan's
managers, and that's the connection of course, but it's obvious that there's a lot of good help going around in the R-and-
B field, and the guys were in good hands with this smoking
Motown singer.

He's got some good stuff out there, Montell has, but my
personal favorite is his very first, *This Is How We Do It* from
1995.

Some critics seem to prefer the next one, though: *More*. . . .
In any case, Montell Jordan is a good singer to listen to if
you really want some more intense R and B, done with all of
today's amazing production values.

All of 98° would heartily recommend him as one of their
mentors—even if he's not all that much older than they are!

BABYFACE

Here's the guy that 98° hasn't worked with yet, but desper-
ately want to.

Not only that, he's from Ohio, too!

Like everyone in 98° but Jeff, Babyface was born in Cincinnati—only about fifteen years before them—as Kenneth Edmonds.

Babyface got his name from famous funkster Bootsy Collins, and if you haven't heard of him it's no wonder, since he's probably better known to the world at large as a producer and musician who's helped stars like Boyz II Men and Whitney Houston and Madonna and Eric Clapton. Nonetheless, if you know R and B, you definitely have heard his records.

Babyface started playing with The Deele, a funk band in the early eighties. There he worked with drummer L. A. Reid. After three records with the Deele, Babyface and Reid moved to Atlanta in 1989, where they set up the LaFace label. They'd learned to produce with their former band, and soon they and their studio became famous. Together, they were responsible for many big hits, including Whitney Houston's *Bodyguard* soundtrack.

After splitting creatively with L. A. Reid, Babyface went on to produce many other records, and now is one of the best-known pop producers.

Babyface also has some excellent CDs of his own out— and it's easy to see how these records influence the 98° sound. For one thing, Babyface's vocals and production—while emphatically R and B—nonetheless tilt more toward smooth middle-of-the-road sounds, and his voice is as much influenced by famous crooners as by soul singers. Also interesting is his use of acoustic guitar in some of his work. If you listen closely to such 98° songs as "Because of You," you'll recognize one important way they are influenced by Babyface.

Look for *The Day* and A *Closer Look* by all means, but my favorite is *The Cool in You*, a terrific record with "When Can I See You," a ballad that 98° would definitely do well.

This guy is where 98° got lots of their *smooth* from.

Let's hope Babyface works on the guys' next album!

BRIAN MCKNIGHT

98° are romantics.

"We probably do best with the ballads," Justin Jeffre has said. Although when Big J starts getting intimate, he's probably using tricks learned from listening to Barry White—but, when Nick and Jeff (and occasionally Drew) take the lead, they're probably using a few tricks learned from the current tenor of romantic R and B, Brian McKnight.

Brian's old brother is Claude McKnight of Take 6, so Brian has always gotten lots of support from that wonderful bunch. However, Brian has always gone less for harmony and more for solo and when his first album came out in 1992, he immediately got a lot of attention, thanks to his sweet readings of quite romantic thoughts and musical feelings. Take 6 and Vanessa Williams helped out, but it was clear from the beginning that, in the frenetic world of jiving, jumping, electrified R and B, another crooner was on the loose, clearly influenced by the greats of the past, like Donny Hathaway, Marvin Gaye and Nat King Cole.

His second album, *I Remember You*, is terrific, but you might want to try his first album, *Brian McKnight*, if only because, along with all those ballads that so clearly influenced our guys, there are lots of great songs, including the outstanding "One Last Cry," a duet with Vanessa Williams that hung out in the top of the pop stratsophere for a long, long time.

If you like the way Nick or Jeff handle those love ballads and you'd like more of the same . . .

Check out Brian McKnight!

ALL SAINTS

If there's one group that makes 98° hot, it's All Saints.

This British quartet is far more R and B than the Spice

Girls, and a group that you might just enjoy, whether or not you like 98°.

For one thing, they not only echo every girl group of pop (all the way back to Martha and Vandellas and The Supremes), they've been listening to plenty of all sorts of R and B. And they can actually harmonize, too, unlike the Spice Girls!

That said, they really are much more R and B than pop, particularly if you think that pop should be bright and bouncy. This has not set well with some churlish critics who don't get some of the smoky grooves these girls lay down. But, really and truly, it does move the R-and-B cause forward into the pop universe!

From the very beginning of the CD, All Saints acknowledge their deep roots, by using a wonderful gospel organ sound in their hit "Never Ever." And, if you've never heard the classic song "Lady Marmalade," their first album would be a good place to start out.

All Saints are Melanie Blatt, Shaznay T. Lewis, Nicky Appleton and Natalie Appleton (yes, the last two are sisters). Shaznay in particular did a lot of the work song writing—but the others all have credits. They're also very interested in an unusual form of R and B called *trip-hop*, which hasn't caught on in the States as much as around the world.

These girls are sort of popular in the United States, but are the absolute toast of the media in Britain.

They also are clearly influenced, it might be added, by another British diva—Sade—who the guys of 98° have a crush on.

Maybe 98° should start dating All Saints, outside their dreams!

It would do both groups good!

JODECI

If it's the dance numbers from the new 98° CD that you like best, then chances are you would like the group known as Jodeci.

The members of 98° often cite this nineties group as an inspirition and, once you get a load of the great harmonizing in the midst of songs that move and dance and hop and groove all at the same time, look no futher than Jodeci.

Like Boyz II Men and 98°, and a number of other R-and-B bands, Jodeci has brothers in it. In this case, two sets of them, Jo Jo and K-Ci Hailey and "Mr. Dalvin" and "DeVante Swing" DeGrate.

Their combination of styles is often called "hip-hop soul" or "New Jack."

The thing about Jodeci is not just that they have the power and dynamics that all types of R-and-B groups need, but they've got terrific vocal powers—sexy, strong and beautiful. These guys have got pipes galore. Obviously strongly influenced individually by the likes of Marvin Gaye and Teddy Pendergrass, collectively they have rich harmonic values that really sell their songs.

Probably the best bet for an album by Jodeci—and I think that 98° would agree with me here—would be their very first, *Forever My Lady*. Not only is it a hot record throughout, it also has "Come and Talk to Me," a song that stayed at number one for a solid thirty weeks on the R-and-B charts, and lingered at the pop charts for 28, up as high as number 11.

Take a listen to these guys, and you'll get a strong idea as to whom Nick and Jeff of 98° listen to get those soulful passions in their voices!

FIVE

Here's the bottom line:

98° is a great white R-and-B group that has worldwide

appeal. Although they certainly have found fans among the folk who adore Backstreet Boys and 'N Sync, they have their particular fans who appreciate them for just what they are. Ultimately, if they are to have a future in the fickle world of popular music, they'll probably grow and mature in R and B and find an older audience.

Right now, if you really wanted to know what to listen to if you wanted brilliant pop of the type that Backstreet Boys, 'N Sync (and their spiritual ancestors, The Archies, The Jackson Five, Abba, Ace of Base, Menudo, New Kids on the Block and others) pursue, a good bet—and one that 98° would agree with, would be Five.

Five, as you may recall, is the group that beat 98° in the poll for best new group in the Smash Hits tour of England. This doesn't mean that they're better than 98°. They are just different, and probably more geared to a British pop audience, at that.

Still, they are so much closer to true black music than BB and Sync, along with top, modern European production, it's a heady brew. What happens here is some pretty decent rapping along with the hip-hop sounds. Mixed with memorable melodies (something that rap's not necessarily known for) the result is pretty darned wonderful, giving it another edge to keep it contemporary, and yet with enough pop gloss. Also, these guys have a secret weapon—a sweet taste of honest-to-God pop reggae for a nice variation. You can't listen to "It's the Things You Do" without thinking of the blissful heights of UB40. What a great song! And, if you haven't heard "When the Lights Go Out!" then you didn't listen to the radio last year!

These guys are young, too, and their voices are younger. While 98° are turning into some great singers, they'll never quite have that special teenage sound these guys can conjure.

Ranging from 16 to 21 years old, Five consist of Sean Conlon, Scott Robinson, J. Brown, Abs Breen and Rich Neville.

The interesting thing about Britain is that it's a true melting pot of music—and it has a strong black heritage as well.

Here, the rich history of black music comes in different flavors that have touched the British culture. Still, as anyone who's listened to British pop or British blues for the past thirty-five years, the Brits are extreme fans of black American music, and are an important market for American black artists.

With the help of many top producers (including the incredible Dennis Pop, who Motown really should get in to work with 98° for their next album), these guys are my favorite teen artists of the day and their first album, *Five*, is a treasure.

Like 98°, they've also done some writing work. Like the Beatles—who got started doing their own form of black music and rock and roll—these guys may be the ones who, in the future take modern R and B and transform pop into the massive cultural phenomenon it was in the sixties.

98° and Rising— Groove by Groove

The company line on the second CD by 98° is that the general feeling was that since their first CD had so many ballads on it, the second should be more dance oriented.

However, the truth is that there are plenty of ballads on the second CD (along, of course, with some lively tunes easy to shake the old booty to) but both ballads and danceable numbers are, well, poppier. While the catchy "Invisible Man" perked up alot of radio waves, the rest of the CD, with its more trad modern R-and-B styling, just didn't find the audience that Motown was looking for.

R and B is a many-splendored thing, though, and there's plenty of room to move, plenty of dance floor to groove.

If 98° started out 25 percent boy band, the feedback from audiences showed what the folks out there wanted. So, as multitalented as the group is, this CD is probably closer to about 75 percent boy band.

However, the Motown arsenal is huge and, while this CD seems more pure pop than the first, the vocal stylings, production values and general air remain pure and true to the R-and-B tradition that both the famous record company and the blue-eyed soul guys are so dedicated to.

It's a more cohesive record in that sense than its predecessor, a CD that you can listen to over and over, and get a kick out of each time, without having to program out any of the songs on your player.

Let's look at it song by song!

Haven't got it? Silly you! Go out, buy it, then get back here—and we'll see what each song does, and maybe get some thoughts from the group on each tune.

Don't worry. I'll wait.

INTRO

Produced by 98°

Recording Engineer: Steve Igner

Recorded at Unique Recording, New York, New York/Mixed by Mick Guzauski/Mix Engineer: Tom Bender/Mixed at Barking Doctor

Recording/Mount Kisco, New York

You can't help but feel as though these guys were just goofing around on this one. It's not really a song at all, just a kind of playful radio announcement of the Orson Welles "War of the Worlds" variety—only Martians aren't landing, it's 98° humming down for a landing!

Against a backdrop of air-raid alarms, a woman with a vaguely British-accented voice announces the rising of temperatures around the world to—

Oh dear. Now what number was that?

Anyway, it's a bit silly—you just kind of wonder what else the guys horsed around with that day that didn't make it onto the CD!

HEAT IT UP!

Written by 98°, Mark Adams, Steve Arrington, Mark Hicks, Thomas Lockett, Raymond Turner, Daniel Wester and Starleana Taylor

Produced by Poke and Tone for Trackmasters ENTERTAINMENT, Inc.

Vocals produced and arranged by 98°

Background vocals: Latoya Dugan, Sylvia Duggin and Ta-
neka Duggin (Off Limits)
Bass: Kern Brantley
Recording Engineer: Jason Goldstein Recorded at The Hit
Factory, New York, New York
Mix Engineer: Rich Travali

Did you say you wanted to dance?

Well, nothing like a little funk to get the party going!
Funk, of course, is nothing without a bass line, and Wow!,
this number has got plunky bass to spare.

Moving along to the percolating bass, Nick trades lead
back and forth with Jeff, while the other guys sing along in
the background. But what's the use dancing without some
girls! Off Limits ladies provide the call-and-response backup
vocals, while goodies like strings and interesting percussion
bounce out of the Trackmasters grab bag, including samples
from the Slave recording "Just a Touch of Love."

This isn't just catchy, it's positively feverish, its lyrics al-
luding to the 98° theme and generally pumping up the volume
and thumping out the syncopated beat.

It's a winner, too, and a fine opener.

One of the things that the guys are so proud of is that they
wrote more material for this CD. Here's a good example of
how they can put the "fun" into funk.

Can't wait for the extended dance mix!

If She Only Knew

Written by Chris Farren and Gordon Chambers
Produced by Dane DeViller and Sean Hosein/Coproduced by
98°
All Programming and Arranging: Sean Hosein and Dane
DeViller
Electric Bass: Brian Newcombe
Classical Guitar: Dane DeViller

Recording Engineer: Steve Smith

Recorded at Banana Toons, Vancouver, British Columbia and Blue Wave, Vancouver, British Columbia/Mixed at Barking Doctor Recording, Mount Kisco, New York.

Well, if this is a dance number, it's gotta be cheek to cheek under the moonlight with candles wavering in the background and the smell of cologne wafting in the air.

Nick croons lead here, with the other guys at first just singing along way deep in the mix. But then, for the first time on the disc, the trademark rich, smooth harmonies of 98° warmly surround the listener and—ah—it's so nice!

This simple but effective ballad could almost be a follow-up to "Was it Something I Didn't Say?" Nick complains that maybe if his love only knew how he felt, she wouldn't have left him!

Beautiful melody here, simple production with tasty and tasteful layering of instruments showcasing Nick's sad confession. But, for me, it's the boys' stirring harmonies that really set this one apart from the flock. Justin's voice particularly shows its subtle importance.

I say: Top-ten single!

I Do (Cherish You)

Written by Keith Stegall and Dan Hill
Produced by Keith Thomas for Yellow Elephant Music, Inc.
Keyboard and Bass: Keith Thomas
Drum Programming: Mark Hammond
Guitars: Gordon Kennedy
Recording Engineer: Bill Whittington
Recorded at The Bennett House, Franklin Tennessee

Here's an interesting number, one of the sweetest on the CD and another slow song during which to sway back and forth cheek to cheek with your honey.

Originally a country hit for Mark Willis, it's particularly interesting to hear how a nice melody can cross genres. Instead of the hiccups and yodels and twang of country singing, Jeff here gives the song the R-and-B, Lionel Richie treatment. It's R-and-B lite—modified soul that works astonishingly well, as the other guys do their usual splendiferous job on backing vocals.

"No matter what, the ballads are definitely our strong point," says Justin in an *iMusic* interview on the Web. "We are always suckers for great love songs."

One of the great things about this CD is that there's absolutely no filler. All the songs sound nice, and it's great to hit a place which, on many records, groups place their weaker material and instead find something like this.

FLY WITH ME

Written by 98°, S. P. Michel, Jerry Duplessis, Stig Anderson, Bjoern Ulvaues and Benny Anderson
Produced by Pras Michel for RCE
Co-produced by Jerry "Wonder" Duplessis for RCE.
Vocals produced and arranged by 98°
Recorded at The Hit Factory, New York, New York

Here's another one the guys are particularly proud of, not just because they turn in a sterling performance, but because they helped to write it. It's much faster than the previous two cuts, but still not as totally funked-out and rocked up as the opener.

The famous producer Pras Michel (and Fugees member) worked on this one. If you listen closely you can here a sample from Abba's famous hit "Dancing Queen." Probably not, though, since they played with it so much, it's almost unrecognizable.

"It was a blast from beginning to end," Nick reported to *iMusic*. "Pras was very funny and kept the session very loose. He was totally open to our ideas."

Famous musician Wyclef was responsible for the standout guitar parts on the tune. The prominent atmosphere is hip-hop, although a low-key and smooth brand of that tasty flavor.

Here Jeff and Nick trade lead vocals much in the way they do in the album's big hit so far, "Because of You." It takes a while to recognize the difference in their voices, but then you realize that, yes indeed, Jeff's voice does go higher than Nick's, while Nick prefers to get maximum warmth and feeling out of the mid-range of notes.

Again, Justin and Drew excel at background support. Flawless.

STILL

Written by 98°, Dane DeViller and Sean Hosein
Produced by Dane DeViller and Sean Hosein
Co-produced by 98°
All programming: Sean Hosein and Dane DeViller
Guitar: Dane DeViller
Recorded at Banana Toons, Vancouver, British Columbia
Mixed at Barking Doctor Recording, Mount Kisco, New York

Here's another romantic song that just won't quit going around your head once you've heard it for a while. 98° helped write it but, again, the team that was responsible for "Invisible Man," Dane DeViller and Sean Hosein, added their songwriting talents and their brilliant production style to the song. DeViller also adds some tasteful acoustic guitar.

This is a unique song on this album because, although, as is often the case, Nick starts off with the lead, from time to time Drew takes over. Word is that when he steps out to croon his lead notes during concert renditions of this song, the audience goes nuts.

"Still," in my opinion, is just as fine a tune as "Invisible Man." The lyrics aren't quite as memorable perhaps, but that's okay. If I were calling the shots, I'd pick this one for the next single. Whenever it comes out as a single, though, it's going to head straight up the charts, I promise you!

BECAUSE OF YOU

Written by Anders Bagg, Arntor Birgisson, Christian Karlson
  and Patrick Tucker
Produced by Bagg, Bloodshy and Arntor for Murlyn Music
Guitar: Patrick Tucker
Violin: Mattia Johanson
Cello: Bearta Soderberg
Recorded at Chung King Studios, New York, New York and
  Murlyn Studios, Stockholm, Sweden

The rollicking "True to your Heart" didn't quite hang in
for the long haul on the charts, so it must have been a relief
to the bigwigs at Motown/Polygram when "Because of You"
lit up the top ten Billboard singles charts for weeks and weeks
and helped give this album the needed boost to get it up into
parking orbit on the album charts.

Here's another song that's somehow both mellow and
danceable. In fact, if you've seen the guys in concert or on
TV you can also see that they've developed a nice dance
routine to this one à la Four Tops or Temptations. (Come to
think of it, there's a slight touch of the former's great, great
"My Girl" in the main melody and the harmony.) The strings
are, in fact, done in the classic Motown style that makes for
such a beautiful and stirring song. And the arrangements!
Oooh la la!

The producers have a fine blend of sounds back and forth
here, featuring a great acoustic guitar lead way forward in the
mix.

My only problem with the song is the silly slide whistle
sound that—um, pops up from time to time. To these ears, it
makes a great pop song lean toward "bubblegum" territory.

Still, you can't argue with the figures and, when the guys
go into their really stirring harmonies, you see why they say
that although they certainly have been influenced by many

vocal groups, they have their own particular and unique sound.

This song will play on radio forever.

GIVE IT UP (INTERLUDE)

Written by 98°
Produced by 98°
Recording engineer: Steve Igner
Recorded at Unique Recording, New York, New York
Mixed at Barking Doctor Recording, Mount Kisco, New York
    Yikes!

After a full half CD of striking songs, the guys are relaxed and confident and ready for their specialty: *A cappella*.

"Give It Up" is a short combination of modern R and B and old-fashioned fifties doo-wop. While Jeff makes a tenor request that his girlfriend give up trying to break his heart, the others do pure nonsense-syllable background harmonies, with Justin way out there with a bobbing bass line that just doesn't quit. They sound good here, with the split-second timing and precision that takes your breath away.

After the tune is done, the guys break up laughing, showing what a great time they have in the studio.

This was also done at Unique Studios, just like that siren number that tops the CD. Those sessions must have quite a blast! 98° is clearly enjoying themselves and, although it shows throughout the album, it particularly shines here.

DO YOU WANNA DANCE?

Written by 98°, Jean Claude Olivier, Samuel Barnes, Boter
    Bell, James Taylor, George Brown, Ronald Bell, Charles
    Smith, Rober Mickens and Eumit Deodato
Produced by Poke and Tone for Trackmasters Entertainment,
    Inc.

Vocals Produced and Arranged by 98°
Recording Engineer: Jason Goldstein
Recorded at The Hit Factory, New York, New York

When you see Trackmasters on a CD, read Dance Number.

Poke and Tone know how to lay down a groove and keep it grooving.

From the opening twangy electric Curtis Mayfield–like guitar (think *Shaft*), thumpy synthesized bass line and seventies string section, you know you're in classic funk dance territory. What distinguishes this, again, are the mellow and flowing vocals in the fine gospel call-and-response that the guys do so well. Jeff warbles above it all winningly, punctuated by some nice horns.

Finally, Justin does a solo—well, sort of. He has a verse or two, in a monotone, asking his partner onto the dance floor in a laid-back manner.

Yes, indeed, another dance number, but not a high-speed thing—just a cruise into mellow. This will get your feet going, though, whether at a disco or a pajama party.

Oh, yes. There's a sample in here from the famous Kool and the Gang hit, "Get Down on It."

Yay, Trackmasters!

TRUE TO YOUR HEART (WITH STEVIE WONDER)

Written by Matthew Wilder and David Zippel
Produced and arranged by Matthew Wilder
Additional vocals: Stevie Wonder
Recording Engineer: Phil Keffel and Chris Fogel
Recorded at Record One, Van Nuys, CA and The Record Plant, Los Angeles, California
From the Walt Disney Motion picture *Mulan*

Why, oh why, was this song not a number-one hit?

When Jay Leno asked Stevie Wonder how he got involved with this song, he answered that he'd been hired originally to play harmonica, but then liked the song enough to do vocals.

Well, with the brilliant Stevie's harmonica and distinctive vocals, this is a Wonder Show. The soul legend simply takes the wheel of the song and puts the pedal to the metal. 98° do a pretty good job of hanging on, though, with Nick starting things off and then the group doing the backup fills and choruses. Toward the end, Justin's big bass comes through effectively.

"When they sent the tape to us at home," Nick told the *iMusic* website, "I was almost in tears listening to it. It was an awesome feeling to hear your voice with Stevie Wonder, exchanging riffs and singing harmony parts together. It was completely unreal!"

This is rather an atypical song compared to the rest of CD—basically it's Disney pop pumped up by Stevie Wonder that turns into a showcase for our guys.

But it sure is a gas!

To Me You're Everything

Written by Anders Bagge, Laila Bagge, Jocellyn Gueridon Mathieus, Maurice White, Eduardo Del-Barrio and Verdine White

Produced by Bag for Murlyn Music

All instruments: Bag

Recorded at Murlyn Studios, Stockholm Sweden and Chung King Studios, New York, New York

Soul Train, watch out!

This dance number has plenty of locomotion.

Jeff's in the lead on this one, but Nick comes in from time to time to add his two cents. Even though it's got a danceable beat, and the trademark back and forth between the 98° foursome, what sets this apart is that it's got a really catchy melody. Jeff's high voice comes in handy, and delivers some nice shivery pop tingles but, ultimately, it's the song itself that stands out the most, perhaps to the contributions of Maurice

White, he of the marvelous Earth, Wind and Fire. As though a nice melody weren't enough, though, a sample from Earth, Wind and Fire's "Fantasy" is included.

Sweet.

THE HARDEST THING

Written by Steve Kipner and David Frank
Produced and Arranged by David Frank and Steve Kipner
Additional production by 98°
Trumpet: Dr. Ray
Keyboards: David Frank
Cello: Stephen Erdody
Recorded at Soundtrack Studios, New York, New York
Mixed at Barking Doctor Recording, Mount Kisco, New York

This ballad has been pegged as the single to follow the smash hit "Because of You."

While it wouldn't be my choice, the decision was actually made by a vote of a large number of 98° fans on the Web.

It's one of those "I'm breaking up with you, baby, 'cause I love you so much" which, sorry, I just can't buy. True, the guys are in there selling it for all they are worth, particularly Nick and Justin. Nick's vocals are so incredibly breathy and sexy that it sounds like he's saying hello rather than goodbye, and Justin gets to do his Barry White Junior bits.

True, it's pretty and it fits in well with the rest of the CD and I wouldn't kick it off my programmer . . .

But still . . . "Still" would be my pick!

SHE'S OUT OF MY LIFE

Written by Tom Bahler
Produced by 98°
Co-produced by Devon Diere for 98° Music, Inc.

Arranged by Devon Biere for 98° Music, Inc.

Recorded at 10th Ave Sound, Nashville, Tennessee and Sixth
  Avenue Sound, Nashville, Tennessee

Mixed at Barking Doctor Recording, Mount Kisco, New York

"That's how we started out singing," says Drew of this final cut. "So that's a sound that we're definitely comfortable with."

"She's Out of My Life," of course, is a song that Michael Jackson sang so successfully.

It's a song that 98° sang way back to get through doors before they got signed, and you can see why they got signed, all right.

It's all 98° here—four guys doing classic four-part harmony. At first, with Nick doing the lead and the other guys doing background, this version of "She's Out of Life" sounds like pure fifties harmony. Think "Mr. Sandman" and the like. And you can believe that these guys have been in barbershop quartets and doo-wop groups. Of course, what is immediately apparent is the polish.

As soon as Nick kicks in with the R-and-B intonations and the song stars to groove and swing a bit, though, we're back in 98° territory and a wonderful one it is.

Of all the pop groups out now, no one is doing this kind of stuff, and 98° simply excels.

"I get goose bumps every time I hear it," says Drew. "The harmonies are just amazing."

Too true.

A wonderful way to end a Stevie Wonderful CD.

98° and Rising may ultimately be considered by snobs a pop confection with a heavy ladling of pure R and B and heavenly voices. But the snobs are probably just like the rest of us 98° fans.

They're playing the darn CD over and over again!

98°: THE LAUNCH CD, CROON BY CROON

The interesting thing about 98° is that it's really, really not a pop group.

It's a pure R-and-B group.

If, by some odd quirk of fate, Nick, Jeff, Justin and Drew don't become even bigger than Backstreet Boys and 'N Sync, they can always just go on back to rhythm and blues.

Evidence: their first CD.

Sure, there's a lot of pop luster—witness "Invisible Man." But at its core, it's R and B.

You can almost imagine the meeting at Motown when the producers and group were discussing what to do for the first CD.

"Well, fellas—you can do a Boyz II Men sorta thing, right? We at Motown know from R and B. So we hear all these groups—these Alley Boys, and Kitchen Sink and BoizeOne. . . . Hey! They're hits. Their doin' R and B. You guys—you do R and B! We'll get lotsa R and B guys, fix you up real good!"

Of course, marketing wise, the producers didn't seem to quite get the fact that although R and B is the flavor of the moment in popular bands, the emphasis is always on the pop aspect. That is, shiny, catchy, easygoing songs that sound real good on the radio. This has always been the case and always will be the case.

With sales in mind, the guys at Motown wised up plenty for the second album, which glitters and glistens and has plans for world domination.

But, for all that, and as crazy as I am about that CD, I honestly like the first 98° album just as much.

Here's why, song by song.

Intro

Written by 98° and Bernard Grubman
All Instruments: Bernard Grubman
Recorded and Mixed at Soundtrack Studios, Inc. New York,
    New York by Paul Logus
    Against a backdrop of a foretaste of the gorgeous ''Completely,'' Justin introduces the band and does his Barry White
sexy deep-voiced thing, talking of passion and romance in
store and proudly announcing that something great is happening.
    Seductive and fun, this kinda draws the line in the sand.
    Boy bands, it seems to say: Yeah, you can warble some
and you know your tenor from your baritone bits—but do
you have the soul it really takes?
    We do!
    Come on in and take a listen.

Come and Get It

Written by Montell Jordan
Produced by Montell Jordan for Mo Swang Production
Keyboards: Shep Crawford
Additional Keyboards: Jazzy D.
Vocal arrangements: Montell Jordan and Shep Crawford
Female Vocals: Kim Morrow
Recorded at Paramount Recordings, Los Angeles, California
    and Desert Moon Studios, Anaheim, California by Anne
    ''Auntie Mae'' Catalino and Greg Montgomery
Mixed at Soundtrack Studios, New York, New York by Chad
    Elliott and Prince Charles
    Justin starts this number off, proudly announcing that this
is Motown here. This is the real stuff!

And real stuff it is!

As you may recall, the guys' manager, Paris D'Jon, was co-manager for the Motown artist Montell Jordan and, in fact, they opened for him quite a few times when they hooked up with D'Jon and company.

Montell returned the favor with a great, great number that cooks and simmers in a definite nighttime R and B way. If anything, it's just a little too hot for pop, with double entendre lyrics and a female vocal straight out of an R-rated movie. It smokes and shimmers, though, with fine production values that would become the rule for 98° songs. Nick introduces his breathy sexy vocals, while the other guys do the backups (Justin happy to let you know he's the bass part) and it gets a bit steamy and panty and sultry.

In short, it's great but, if you're young, you might just want to wait to grow up some to listen to this one.

Ultramodern lounge R and B—a smoothie.

INVISIBLE MAN

Written by Dane DeViller, Sean Hosein and Steve Kipner
Produced by Dane DeViller and Sean Hosein
Acoustic Guitar: Dane DeViller
Electric Bass: James Genus
Recorded at Chung King Studios, New York, New York, The Hit Factory, New York, New York and Soundtrack Studios, New York, New York, by Kenny Ortiz, Glen Marchese and Mikael Ifverson
Mixed at Barking Doctor

98° have to love this one.

It's the song that first got them the kind of attention they needed to get anywhere good in show business.

It's also actually the first song they recorded for Motown, and something they say that set the tone for the whole first CD.

When this song came out, *Billboard* magazine called 98°

charismatic, and said of "Invisible Man": "Not only are their vocals several crucial notches above the competition, but this sweet, shuffling groove ballad has lyrics that are as clever as they are romantic and charming. Try and shake the hook from your mind after one listen. It is virtually impossible."

Jeff and Nick start their tradition of trading off vocals here, with Nick providing the smoky lower mournings about being ignored by an admired one, with Jeff's high tones swooping around in the Mariah Carey skyways. And Justin, of course, is irrepressible, getting a moment or two to throb out his heartache.

Finally, there is a taste of the fab foursome doing a doo-wop take on the song, which leaves the listener of the CD hungry for more.

Beyond the hooks, the main attraction of the song is the universal experience of having feelings for someone—and getting ignored. You can't help but want to comfort these lovelorn guys but, in their pretty, pretty song, you get some comfort from these kind of hurts your poor heart has suffered.

This tune got up as high as number 12 on the *Billboard* Hot 100 and was a hit around the world.

A classic from the git-go.

WAS IT SOMETHING I DIDN'T SAY

Written by Diane Warren
Produced by Daryl Simmons for Silent Partner Production, Inc.
Acoustic Guitars: Dick Smith
Drums and Percussion: Steve Meeder
Bass: Ronnie Garrett
Keyboards and Drum Programming: Daryl Simmons
Engineered and Mixed by Thom "TK" Kidd
Recorded and Mixed at Silent Sound Recording Studios, Atlanta, Georgia

Another sad and regretful ballad that perhaps could have

been pushed back into the CD further, since we're just drying our eyes after "Invisible Man."

Still, it's a goodie, and it's surprising that the song in its single form didn't quite make the impact that "Invisible Man" did.

Jeff starts this one off, moaning and groaning about not telling his honey—gone now, natch—that he loved her. Still, this one is a nice, swaying song to get close to a dance partner with. The guys pull out their high range, particularly well on this one, still not going to a Bee Gees sort of falsetto, but getting up there anyway. Nick here shows more of some of his British soul-crooner roots, sounding a bit more like George Michael than usual, to good effect.

A real goodie, this song will be in the guys' act for quite some time to come.

TAKE MY BREATH AWAY

Written by Steve Gissette and Maxx Frank
Produced by Steve Grissette and Maxx Frank
Keyboards: Maxx Frank
Keyboard Overdubs: Nathan Maxwell
Bass: Tony "Downtown" Brown
Acoustic Guitar: Craig McCreary
String Arrangements: Maxx Frank
Mixed at Unique Recording Studios, New York, New York

A little faster tempo, but still laid back and mellow. Once this one pours from the speakers, you know you are truly in leather-couch and cruise-control land.

This one sounds a little like Barry Gibb of the Bees Gees might have written it, with Robin and Maurice switching off high voices and putting in backups, but it's pretty much still orbiting around Luther Vandross, with a few patented modern R-and-B fills and frills.

A nice song, but after three ballads in a row, you feel like 98° aspiration is to become lounge lizards.

HAND IN HAND

(Duet with LeShanda Reese)
Written by Mario Winans and Kenneth Hickson
Produced by Mario Winans for D.A.R.P. Inc.
All Instruments: Mario Winans
Recorded and Mixed at Soundtrack Studios, Inc. New York,
  New York
  Okay! Okay!
  Yep, another ballad, but this one has the smarts to put in a great female voice (LeShanda Reese).
  A terrific melody, with a nice catchy chorus, really makes this one stand out, and LeShanda Reese's Whitney Houston–gospel high notes really bring out the best in 98°.
  Male and female duos go way back in R and B. (Marvin Gaye and Tammie Terrell, Ike and Tina Turner, Ashford and Simpson, Michael Jackson and Paul McCartney. . . . oops, strike that last one) and here's a stirring example that 98° can well hold up that tradition.
  One of my favorites on the CD.

INTERMOOD

Written by 98° and Bernard Grubman
All instruments: Bernard Grubman
Recorded and Mixed at Soundrack Studios, Inc. New York,
  New York
  This is actually just another snippet of the forthcoming "Completely" as also foreshadowed in the Intro, but it feels really nice, with those irresistible 98° harmonies doing *a cap-*

pella with Justin way in the forefront of the mix.

A nice device for continuity!

DREAMING

Written by Montell Jordan, Shep Crawford and Professor Funk

Produced by Montell Jordan, Shep Crawford and Professor Funk for Mo Swang Productions

Vocal arrangement: Montell Jordan and Shep Crawford

Keyboards: Shep Crawford

Piano: Montell Jordan

Bass and Guitar: Professor Funk

Recorded at Paramount Recordings, Los Angeles, California and Desert Moon Recordings, Anaheim, California

Recorded by Anne "Auntie Mae" Catalino and Greg Montgomery

Mixed at the Hit Factory, New York, New York

This one's got bits from "Shimmy Shimmy Ya" by the Wu-Tang Clan.

Montell Jordan is at the producing helm again, and he wrote the song with a couple of other guys, so you know you're in sturdy R-and-B territory. This has got lots of good stuff in it, including what sounds like an unusual lead from Drew (although no credit is given). Nice computer-game sounds, unusual piano bit by Montell, and a cool guitar riff from Professor Funk. After cruising through most of the song, though, the guys break out into nice complex vocal arrangements—and then Justin goes into one of the very few raps on 98° songs.

So, if you like your rap and you're looking for some in 98°, you'll find a touch here—not much, but just enough to whet the appetite for future forays into that form.

This one is definite proof that 98° can hang with the big boys.

HEAVEN'S MISSING AN ANGEL

Written by Christopher A. Stewart, Sean K. Hall, Sam Salter
   and Tab
Produced by Tricky and Sean for Red Zone Entertainment
Keyboards: Tricky and Sean for Red Zone Entertainment
Recorded at Boss Productions, Atlanta, Georgia by Tricky
   and Sean
Mixed at Silent Sound, Inc, Atlanta, Georgia by Kevin "KD"
   Davis
   This one has special importance for Nick, since he and his
little brother lost their grandmother the night they recorded
it. They think of her especially whenever they sing it.
   Sounds to me like Jeff is on lead with this one, but the
other guys have got a harmony mix that is a little further out
front than usual, with Jeff emoting in the background.
   Another sad one, plus some nice acoustic guitar. (For some
reason, have you noticed that there's a heck of a lot of acoustic guitar on 98° songs? Tasteful guitar, too.)
   The arrangement here is tasteful, with spare background
that emphasizes the guys lead and harmony work. This seems
to be the hallmark of the 98° production philosophy—don't
hide these guys' fantastic vocals!

I WASN'T OVER YOU

Written by Christopher A. Stewart, Sean K. Hall and Tab
Guitar: Tommy Martin
All other Instruments: Tricky and Sean
Recorded at Boss Productions, Atlanta Georgia by Tricky and
   Sean, Mixed at Silent Sound Studios, Inc. Atlanta, Georgia
   by Kevin "KD" Davis

At about this point in the CD, you begin to understand why Motown and the guys made the decision to salt the next CD with faster dance tunes.

This is another ballad that's perfect for a romantic back and forth with your beloved, but is so relaxing that if you're just sitting by the fire with your romantic baby, you might just fall asleep!

Fortunately, a subdued rock-guitar break toward the end comes in to shake things up a little bit and move away from being so laid back.

COMPLETELY

Written by 98° and Bernard Grubman
Produced by 98° for 98° Music Inc.
Co-produced by Bernard Grubman
All instruments: Bernard Grubman
Recorded and mixed at Soundtrack Studios, Inc. New York, New York by Paul Logus

Here's the song that the guys have been teasing us with the whole album, and it's a fine one.

Turns out it's got a big Latin beat, this one, for a really nice change of pace and a definite dance-floor turn. Jeff does the lead vocal chores, and he's a Latin lover all right, swinging the melody back and forth with panache and passion.

But of course, its those—oooh!—warm and smooth background vocals that make this a distinctly 98° song. The guys always insist that although they've certainly been influenced by lots of different music and musicians, ultimately they've got their own unique sound.

"Completely" has a lot of pride stamped all over it because not only did Jeff, Justin, Nick and Drew work on the production—they've also got writing credits on the song. But, above all, this song really shows off the unique vocal blend, identity and cool-yet-warm style that is the 98° trademark.

Don't Stop the Love

Written by Christopher A. Stewart, Sean K. Hall and Robin
. Thicke
Produced by Tricky and Sean for Boss Productions, Inc.
All Instruments: Tricky and Sean
Recorded at Boss Productions, Atlanta, Georgia by Tricky
and Sean
Mixed at Silent Sound Studios, Inc. Atlanta, Georgia by
Kevin 'KD' Davis

This could be a Janet Jackson song but, then again, Janet
can't sing tenor or bass.

Of course, Nick Lachey can't sing soprano or alto either,
but he does a fine turn at the vocal leads here, particularly
the leaps at the end.

"Don't Stop the Love" has lots of modern R and B in-
strumental sounds, including a mellow bass line and a nice
high synthesizer bit. And, of course, its harmonies are sweet
and tasty.

Good stuff.

I Wanna Love You

Written by Kenny Greene, Rashad Smith and Armando Colon
Produced by Rashad Smith for Tumblin' Dice Productions,
Inc.
Associate Producer: Armando Colon
Keyboards: Armando Colon
Drum Programming: Rashad Smith
Recorded at: Soundtrack Studios, New York, New York, and
The Hit Factory, New York by Mario Rodriguez

Again, against an understated background, the guys' vocal
mix shines through—and to spectacular effect here.

The groove spikes up to low funk here, and against this mellow percolation, Nick and Jeff let loose a fascinating, satisfying duet a little more reminsient of the singers in the British group Squeeze than anything in R and B.

And here, of course, is one of the reasons that 98° brings something special to the R-and-B tradition. All the producers and writers around them are steeped in R and B, soul, rap, hip-hop and peripheral schools of music. And certainly 98° know Otis Redding from Boy George.

Nonetheless, these guys also bring something from other musics, implicit in their voices. Nick, for example, is a big Journey fan and you can't help thinking that he got some exercise in flexing those vocal chords attempting to imitate Steve Perry.

So, in the big mixing pot that is music, 98° bring their own special combo to the stew.

"I Wanna Love You" is the final triumphant statement of 98° on their freshman testament to blue-eyed R and B.

We're on our way, folks!

And we're gonna be around for a long, groovy, funky and above all, harmonic time!

Websites, Chat Rooms and Fan Club

One of the most amazing results of the Internet and Worldwide Web is how much easier it is to talk to people who have the same interests as you—around the world.

98° fans are popping up everywhere, and many know not just how to navigate the Internet, but how to set up websites.

Of course 98° and Motown are aware of this, so there's an official 98° website:

http://www.98Degrees.com

This is an elegant place, always chock full of info about where the guys are doing appearances, concerts—and when they're on TV. It also has 98° souvenirs for sale—include 98° Gear (coming soon), which is presumably T-shirts or even regular clothing.

(The guys are so cool looking, they really should have their own clothing line, huh?)

As long as you're checking out official websites, you should go to the Motown site—filled with info about the guys, and other great Motown artists—plus more history than we've got here!

http://www.motown.com

My personal favorite of the websites is "Hot 98°":

http://www.geocities.com/Hollywood/Boulevard/9582/index.html

The Webmaster, Krystal, is a dedicated 98° fan—and she's done a wonderful job with this one. Particularly cool are the

"98 Degree Experiences"—contacts fans have had with the group.

Another vital site is the 98° Dimension:

http://members.xoom.com/98degrees/main2.htm

This gets constantly updated and it's got pictures and exclusives galore.

We can't possibly list all the 98° fan sites here, but all you have to do to find most of them quickly is to go to:

http://webring.org/cgi-bin/webring?ring=hot98degrees;
list

This is the 98° Webring, run by the 98° and Rising site and it's pretty amazing. If you can make it here, you can click on sites in the U.S., Canada, England, Hong Kong and Singapore, full of fascinating stuff about the guys.

This ring is also the way you can find your way to the 98° chat rooms on the Web.

Finally, if you don't have access to the Web (or even if you do and want some cool stuff) join:

> The 98° Fan Club
> P.O. Box 31379
> Cincinnati, OH
> 45231

Send a S.A.S.E., and you'll get the details about how much a membership costs, but you'll get a newsletter, pictures, and lots of special treats.

98° fans are special people.

The group treats them well. . . . and they treat each other well, too.

Vital Statistics

THE LOWDOWN ON NICK

FULL NAME:	Nicholas Scott Lachey
BIRTHDATE:	November 9, 1973
BIRTHPLACE:	Harlan, Kentucky
NICKNAME:	L. A. Lachey, Slider, Hollywood
EYES:	Blue
WEIGHT:	185 pounds
HAIR:	Brown
HEIGHT:	Five feet, eleven inches
ASTROLOGICAL SIGN:	Scorpio

PREFERENCES

CHOW:	Barbeque, pizza, steak, Skyline Chili
DRINK:	Yoo Hoo
MOVIE:	*Die Hard*
ACTRESS:	Michelle Pfieffer
ACTOR:	Bruce Willis
MUSIC:	Jodeci, Sade, Boyz II Men, Brian McKnight, Take 6
CLOTHES:	Phat Farm

JEFF FAX

FULL NAME:	Jeffrey Brandon Timmons
BIRTHDAY:	April 30, 1973
BIRTHPLACE:	Canton, Ohio
WEIGHT:	160 pounds
EYES:	Blue
HAIR:	Brown

HEIGHT:	Five feet, eight inches
NICKNAME:	Sugar
VOICE:	Tenor

PREFERENCES

CLOTHES:	Phat Farm
SPORTS:	Football
TEAM:	Dallas Cowboys
FILM:	*The Shawshank Redemption*
ACTRESS:	Salma Hayek
ACTOR:	Robert De Niro
FOOD:	Seafood and steak
COLORS:	Blue, orange

VITAL STATISTICS: JUSTIN!

FULL NAME:	Justin Paul Jeffre
BIRTHDATE:	February 25, 1973
BIRTHPLACE:	Mount Clemens, Michigan

VOICE:	Bass
HEIGHT:	Five feet, ten inches
WEIGHT:	155 pounds
EYES:	Blue
ASTROLOGICAL SIGN:	Pisces

PREFERENCES

CHOW:	Doughnuts, Pizza, Skyline Chili
COLOR:	Blue
SPORTS:	Tennis, soccer
SPORTS TEAMS:	Cincinnati Bengals
MOVIE:	*Braveheart*
ACTRESS:	Reese Witherspoon
ACTOR:	Robert De Niro
COLOR:	Blue
DRINK:	Orange juice
CLOTHES:	Phat Farm, DKNY, Ralph Lauren

THE SKINNY ON DREW

FULL NAME:	Andrew John Lachey
BIRTHDATE:	August 8, 1976
BIRTHPLACE:	Cincinatti, Ohio
VOICE:	Baritone
HEIGHT:	Five feet, six inches
WEIGHT:	148 pounds
NICKNAME:	Sprout
EYES:	Hazel
HAIR:	Brown
SIGN:	Leo

PREFERENCES

DRINK:	Orange juice
CLOTHES:	Tommy Hilfiger
ACTORS:	Mel Gibson, Harrison Ford
MOVIE:	*Braveheart*

ACTRESS: Rene Russo

SONG: "Purple Rain," Prince

PERFORMERS: Prince, Marvin Gaye, Take 6

FOODS: Pizza, doughnuts, junk food

COLOR: Navy blue

Just a Boy Band?

The annals of popular music are littered with groups and singers who were hot for a while, then lost their luster and faded from view, leaving behind a few songs that might linger in memory and become the fodder for oldies radio stations.

Although their novelty and charm are strong at present, aspects of the top male singing groups now—Backstreet Boys and 'N Sync—are exactly the sort of thing a few years down the line that will embarrass their fans.

Thousands of BB fans, for instance, will wake up in college and watch and think, I can't believe that I thought A. J. looked cool in goggles!

Thousands of 'N Sync fans, as their tastes mature, will think back and say, "I can't believe I didn't realize these guys sounded like a silly version of the Pet Shop Boys raiding the lamer pop songs of history!"

Although, in some ways, their lack of gimmicks have so far held back 98° from the heights of pop stardom, this is perhaps for the best in the long run. The word for these guys is mellow, cool, laid back—and classic.

No chair routines. No vinyl trousers. No goofiness here. Just clean-cut good looks, solid singing, tasteful song choices, guy-next-door personalities. True, the fact that Nick and Jeff look better without the shirts on than anyone else in pop (that are allowed to take their shirts off in concert, anyway) hasn't hurt their cause but, for all intents and purposes, they could be nude when they record their songs, and that wouldn't help their voices and songs one bit.

The truth is simply that 98° has wisely decided to put their faith in their music. Music has lifted them up their entire lives, and you can hear the joy in their expressions of it—and their love for the traditions that they continue—and as they stamp their own identities on it.

How do they really feel about being called a boy band?

"I don't get offended by it," says Nick in *Pop Star*. "I just think we're deeper than that. Boy bands are more dancers and performers than singers. We pride ourselves singing live. It's singing first."

Think about it. These guys have only been singing together for a few years. Now they've got the top trainers and producers in the R-and-B world teaching them what they know—and they're getting plenty of show business practice. Voices are things that get better with training and age. Vocal groups are better the more practice they have.

98° are going to around for a long, long time.

About the only one who might do solo records, I think, is Nick (although Jeff might have the stuff, I think he prefers singing with a group). Anyway, it's a tradition in today's R-and-B world to go out and work here and there in other bands . . . just as long as you come back to your home group regularly.

On the other hand, 98° have a committment.

What happens if someone leaves the group, an interviewer asked in Asia?

"They die," Jeff returned.

He was just kidding, of course, but nonetheless it's as a group that 98° is making its mark and it's as a group that they will continue being known.

What's next for them?

Well, they'll probably do the Christmas album thing. That seems to be almost traditional, since next Christmas season *98° and Rising* could well still be on the charts and a Christmas album wouldn't hurt its sales.

Will they call it *Christmas in Cincinnati*?

Whatever, you can count on it being a good one. I can't wait for some good doo-wop blue-eyed soul *a cappella!*

In any case, Motown is solidly behind them.

In a recent special issue of *Face in Pop*, a Motown representative is quoted as saying:

"We believe that 98° can be a major band in the years to come. They have everything going for them—the looks, the sounds, the determination. I think they've only begun to show a fraction of what they can do. We're all so incredibly excited about their future."

Predictions?

Well, in a year or two, I think the guys will start playing their instruments at shows, and maybe in the recording studio.

Also, they'll be writing more songs and, thus, the 98° sound will develop.

Look also for more duets with major legends of R and B. Who can't say exactly who, but I'm sure it will happen.

Also, look for them doing more songs that are tied into movies and television shows. (This will not only help them become better known, but it will widen the range of their music. Why do I say this? Well, Seagram's just bought Polygram, which owns Motown. Seagrams also owns Universal, which does lots of movies and TV shows.)

Also they'll probably pop up on TV shows and in movies. Although they aren't actors yet, they've got the looks and the pizzazz, so that might be an avenue. Nick and Jeff have been in movies and commercials and they've all acted on *City Guys* . . . so who knows?

Most of all, though, 98° stand on the solid rock of R and B, a rock planted deeply in tradition—gospel, blues and soul—music that will remain to comfort and guide and inspire for a long, long time. Although the classic peformers will always be no further away than our CD players, people always need fresh intepretations of the vitality and life that music can bring, along with the fresh innovations unique to our own time.

Music makes you feel good.

Music lets you feel.
And, if with 98°, you always tend to feel a little warm . . .
Well, it can be a cold world out there.
It's nice to have some good friends around with some fire.